REFLECTIONS

Between the Lines

The Healing of the Vietnam Generation

TURNER PUBLISHING COMPANY
PADUCAH, KENTUCKY

PHOTO CREDITS

Photographs in this book are all the work of Janice Goff-LaFontaine,
except the following:
Tim O'Brien and Rob Comstock photographed by Roger LaFontaine
Warren Johnson photographed by Linda Orth Schnobrich
Tim Breen, self-portrait by Tim Breen

My deepest thanks to all of them for their wonderful contributions.

TURNER PUBLISHING COMPANY
412 Broadway • P.O. Box 3101
Paducah, KY 42002
(270)443-0121

Turner Publishing Company Staff:
Randy Baumgardner, Editor
Shelley R. Davidson, Designer

Library of Congress Catalog Card No. 00-102580
ISBN: 1-56311-378-3

Printed in the United States of America.
Additional copies may be purchased directly from the publisher.
Limited Edition

CONTENTS

DEDICATION

This book is dedicated to my husband, Roger, whose experience was the inspiration, and whose love and support made it possible; and to my step-mom Mary Ann, for her love and encouragement to live fully and follow my dreams, and to my Mom and Dad for their unconditional love and support.

Although the cover bears my name, this book truly belongs to all the men and women who served in Vietnam, who risked and forever changed their lives. It belongs to all those whose stories are between its covers, and the thousands of others whose stories wait to be heard.

This photograph of a butterfly landing softly on the open hand of a child was taken in October 1989, the day before my husband and I were married. It was a symbol of the love and gentleness I found with him, and the joy he brought to my life. Three days later, the Loma Prieta earthquake damaged our home and transformed the gentle, even-tempered man I had known for five years, back into a Vietnam soldier in survival mode. His outlook on life and his temperament seemed to change as he endured the flashbacks and memories triggered by this event. He was unable to return to the job he held for more than 20 years. He struggled with depression, anxiety, and anger, culminating in a heart attack in 1993.

This closing of his arteries allowed him to open his heart, and finally resuscitate all the emotions he had buried so long ago, to look his ghosts in the eye, and try not to blink. It has been a long and harrowing journey, but he is finally able to begin healing, to transform his problems into challenges, and his failures into lessons. The butterfly image has now come to represent the fragile, ever-changing nature of life, and the transformation that took place in him, and in every person who served in Vietnam.

I dedicate this image of the delicate beauty of life, of the limitless possibility of change and transformation, to the veterans of the Vietnam war. From the bottom of my heart, thank you, and welcome home.

INTRODUCTION

Transformation; to change the outward form or inner character.

Between the lines on the Vietnam Memorial Wall, are the stories of the veterans who returned, their experience there forever transforming their lives, completely altering their inner makeup, and some times their outward form as well. In this book, they share those stories from their hearts, and ask you to open your heart to see, reflected in their eyes and in their words, how it felt then, and how it feels today. My hope is that this book, like the Vietnam Memorial, will bring healing, both for the veterans, and for the rest of America. As one veteran, Charlie James said, "This is the first time I've been able to talk about it with someone who didn't want war stories, someone who only cared what it cost and how it felt. It feels good to do that." This book asks us all to listen and to care.

We sometimes fail to realize the depth to which war changes people. In the years since their return, each of these men and women has had the daunting task of bringing the person that existed before Vietnam into harmony with the new, and often unwelcome person they saw in the mirror. They are not the media-induced stereotype of the angry guy in jungle fatigues, and in fact, many are not guys, and some did not wear a uniform at all. We may think of the Vietnam vet only as the guys in combat every day; but every person who served there, male or female, in the jungle, in the office, in the hospital or service club, on a ship or in a plane, had a life-changing experience. Each of them is a veteran, and they all did their part; they fought, they healed, they served, they tried to keep themselves and each other alive and sane. They were all afraid, they were all brave, they were all wounded, and they all tried to get on with their lives when they came home.

I began photographing and interviewing Vietnam veterans in my own quest to understand my husband's lingering ghosts. As he struggled with the anger and depression of the teenage boy he was, I was left to wonder what had happened to the happy, even-tempered man I loved, and why a 23-year-old wound would not heal. Had he suddenly gone crazy, was he using it as an excuse for bad behavior? This only brought more anger as he faced questions to which he had no answers, problems he couldn't admit even to himself. To make sense of it all, I began to seek out other Vietnam vets. I wanted to know who they were, what they looked and sounded like now, and if being there still affected their lives too. What I found was that, although some veterans fit the media stereotype, most were people who looked and acted just like the rest of the population, still trying to blend into the society that rejected them. There are some homeless, some mentally ill who never came back from the dark days of Vietnam, but there are also police chiefs, senators, moms, bank presidents, teachers, and people who live next door to you.

Who were these people, these soldiers, and nurses, and volunteers, who went half way around the world to serve their country, back in the days of free love and flower children? Vietnam veterans were the youngest ever, most barely out of high school. They fought and died, at an average age of 19, seven years younger than their fathers who fought in WWII. Nurses, most just out of school, saw the bleakest, most horrifying face of war, day after day, in the mangled boys who could be their little brothers. At a time in their lives when their days should've been filled with concerts and college campuses, and their nights with dates and drive-ins, they were fighting an invisible enemy in primitive and subhuman conditions, in the beautiful and bloody landscape of Southeast Asia. The values of their WWII parents – duty, courage, honor, love of family and country – were what inspired them to go to Vietnam; but once they were there, every value they had, both moral and religious, was challenged, and their only motivation became survival. Every day they wondered if they would make it back, if they'd ever get to do all the things that turning 21 allows, all the things they were too young to do as they trudged these killing fields. They wondered if they would leave in a body bag, or on a stretcher, like so many others they saw. Their emotions intensified beyond comprehension, alternating between fear and rage, and they were possessed by an overpowering determination to survive. They learned to live a life that played out one day at a time. When they came home they were aged beyond their years, hardened and angered by what they had been through, what they had seen and done, and the rejection and hostility of their country.

How did their voyage to this world that most of us can't imagine change them? I discovered that nearly every one of them had stories similar to what my husband was going through, but each with a unique twist. The stories were all the same, yet each was entirely different, as diverse as the people telling them.

But there seemed to be many common threads, weaving all their stories together. Many veterans had similar experiences and feelings, both in Vietnam and after they returned. One major issue, their feeling of being alone, began the day they went to Vietnam, and often continues even today. Most made the long and frightening journey to Vietnam alone, spent their time there feeling alone in an ever-changing rotation of comrades, and returned home, still alone. "When we were there," my husband says, "our biggest fear was that we would die totally alone, with no one who cared or even knew us by our side. Nobody talked to you when you first got there, and you tried not to have close relationships; it was too painful when someone got killed, or even when a buddy rotated out, or you went home and left a buddy behind."

For nurses, this was even more of an excruciating reality. Lily Adams, a triage nurse, remembers, "I got attached even in a the few minutes I had with them; they'd share intimate details...precious memories they want to share before they die. Then they die...and the loss is so painful. I was like a robot by the end of my tour. I totally locked my heart; I didn't want to be hurt anymore."

When veterans returned, hoping to be welcomed back into "the world", their disillusionment festered as they found themselves once again alone, feeling like they didn't fit in. The hero in Vietnam was transformed to heartless killer in his home town. "I was shocked at the anger people had for veterans," says Greg Burham. "People saw us as crazy, baby killers, waiting to go off. I was afraid of being found out, like I was some kind of animal or killer." So he, and almost all the other vets I talked to, hid their identity, and tried to "slide back into normalcy without being noticed". They felt tainted and ashamed.

Most of the image we had of veterans came from the media stereotype. "The media did more to harm veterans than anyone, even Charlie," said Jeffrey Budzis. "At least Charlie was up front about it, and said I got a bullet with your name on it. The media said we love our country, but you guys are evil."

Even nurses and civilian women, who gave only healing and comfort in Vietnam, and did not fit the stereotype, were scorned as being "no better than the soldiers, because they just helped the war continue". When it came to finding a job, they were rejected just as quickly as the men for being Vietnam veterans. Cathleen Cordova, who had a college degree and experience in her field, was denied employment because of her service there. "If it was that hard for me," she says, "think of these poor 18-year-old kids who came back with no training but shooting a machine gun. No wonder they had such a hard time adjusting."

When returning veterans sought help in adjusting, they were repudiated again. Many had severe problems with flashbacks, nightmares, depression, anger, and guilt, and most thought once again, that they were alone since they didn't associate with other vets. When they turned to the VA for help, they were denied. These veterans were suffering from what was called shell shock in WWII, and is now known as PTSD, or Post Traumatic Stress Disorder; but the government said 'it's not our problem', and sent them away to deal with it on their own. For many, this was the kiss-off of death; *more than 100,000 Vietnam veterans have committed suicide.*

The clinical definition of PTSD states that it is "a normal reaction to an abnormal situation", but nobody who experiences the symptoms ever feels their reactions are normal. "I'd just hide in the house with the lights off and cry, feeling like I was going crazy," said Winnie Smith, "I was so scared. I thought they were probably going to institutionalize me, so I was afraid to let anybody see me." Veterans struggled with this for well over 10 years before the VA would admit that there was a connection between PTSD and service in Vietnam. In the 1980's, they finally began to offer treatment for PTSD, and many vets found some measure of relief. For some, it was too late, and they may never come home; the war still wages within them.

For many of us, war and the devastating effect it has on people, is not a reality because we have been fortunate enough to never have to experience it. But for veterans it is not an abstraction, happening to someone else. "If people understood the depth to which you're changed in war, they would not be so quick to support it," says Winnie. "And if they back the government in sending us to war, we shouldn't have to beg for help when we come home."

The VA denied them help because they didn't want to pay the potentially staggering amounts of money involved in disability claims. We denied them acceptance because we couldn't separate the veteran from the war from the government. And we couldn't understand the problems they experienced when they came home, because we weren't there, and it was too frightening to listen to their pain. But we have all experienced traumas in our lives, and when I stopped to examine my own life, I learned an important lesson in empathy.

While I was writing this book, I lost my dear step-mom of 30 years, and my world changed. My usually happy, optimistic nature turned dark, even mean at times. My friends said I sounded and looked different, and I certainly felt different. I was sad beyond words, I was angry, at her, at the doctors, at myself, at anyone I could think of to blame for what was taken away from me. I didn't want to talk to anyone, I lashed out, I cried, I sometimes cried so much I went completely numb. This is my fresh wound, and I suddenly realized I was feeling many of the things veterans told me they felt after the war, the same things I felt 31 years ago when my Mom died, and 20 years ago when my Dad died. These feelings lessen after awhile, but they don't go away. Ever.

So I tried to imagine how the intense emotion I felt on the day of my loved ones death would feel if I had to relive it every single day for a whole year. How would it feel if I had to grieve a death every day, *and* be afraid that I might be the next to die? Or if I wasn't allowed to express my grief at all, or go to the funeral? What would I feel like at the end of that year?

I tried to imagine it, but it was too painful, I knew I couldn't bear it. But that is what these veterans had to endure, and that is why they can never forget. The memories aren't as fresh, so the feelings aren't as intense now, but they will never go away. As you read these stories, remember the most painful thing that ever happened to you, and multiply it by 365 days. Maybe this will allow you to understand, to open your heart to these veterans, to truly feel their experience. As Tim O'Brien says, "War stories are not about war...they are about the human heart". These stories are from their hearts to yours.

The images attempt to capture the sadness, the anger, the fear, the hope, the guilt, the courage, and the gratitude for being alive, that these veterans feel. Many of them have hidden their identities for all of these years, and these photographs represent their "coming out of the closet". The middle-aged eyes of the boys and girls of the Vietnam war implore us not to turn away this time. They invite us into their lives to finally let the wounds heal.

The eyes that look at you in these images, ask you to see, as if for the first time, who the individual called the Vietnam veteran really is. Their words will make you cry, and they will make you smile, and fill you with inspiration, as you marvel at the courage and power of the human spirit, to overcome, and to heal. And that is why this book is in your hands; to help you, to help them, to help our nation, to heal. The healing is long overdue, but it is never too late to open your heart and say, "Thanks."

ROGER LAFONTAINE

Roger grew up with a deep sense of religious and moral values, and knew the war was wrong. When Kent State happened, he almost went to Canada, but he still felt a patriotic duty and a need to avoid bringing shame to his family.

"Vietnam stripped me of all I'd been brought up to believe in; God, the Commandments, everything decent and good. We were young and naive, forced to see and do things no one should ever have to. It was bizarre; I could not drink or vote, but they hand me a gun and say it's OK to kill someone. On a gun truck we were always under fire, always on the alert for an ambush. The constant state of hyper-vigilance, of unimaginable fear, was the worst thing. You could never come down from it. Sometimes I'd get so pumped, I didn't know if I was breathing. Guys got severely injured and didn't even know it until afterward. I remember shooting a machine gun, sobbing, I was so enraged and so terrified."

When he came home, he felt such prejudice, he could not share his experience or his feelings with anyone. He never even told anyone he was there.

"I felt like an ex-con, afraid my past would be discovered. I didn't fit, and I became very introverted, a loner. Everything about me had changed in that one year, but I could never share it with anyone, or proudly say I served my country. I turned off anything to do with Vietnam, and never associated with other vets."

"I left Florida in my van in 1972, and went west. Vietnam left me with no emotions, a dead heart; nothing impressed or surprised me. That trip was like being reborn, seeing for the first time. I felt almost normal. It gave me a new love for my country, a feeling it was worth fighting for. And when I found Colorado, I felt like I had a home. One positive of Vietnam was, it got me out of Florida, gave me a new way of life in Colorado. I ended up going to sea for a living instead of going to school in marine biology as I'd planned, because I could hide at sea. I lived in the mountains and worked at sea, the best of both worlds."

But years of hyper-vigilance and repressed feelings about Vietnam culminated in a heart attack at age 43, and forced all those feelings to the surface.

"Facing the Vietnam ghosts scares me; that was me for my whole adult life, and I don't know what'll be left if I let go of those feelings. But now if I get stressed or angry, I can clearly feel the effects in my body. I take care of everyone else, but find it difficult to give to myself. I guess I still have the feeling I had when I came home from Vietnam, that I'm not worthy, not as good as my peers who didn't go. I hid my identity for so long, I don't even know who 'Me' is anymore, but I'm on a quest to find out. I'm trying to heal those old wounds and turn it into a positive learning experience, to grow from it. Finally meeting and hearing the stories of other vets through this book has been very healing for me. It's comforting to know others share the pain and struggles and to see there is always hope. I think just knowing we are not alone brings healing."

"I realize that I was given a great gift, to survive Vietnam, to come home without any physical scars. Because I was given this gift, I feel it's very important for me to live my life the very best I can, to do something positive. I'm a work in progress, picking up the pieces, trying to heal, and reshape myself into the best I can be. I may never succeed in getting rid of all the ghosts, but I will spend the rest of my life trying."

DIANE CARLSON EVANS

21 years old — Army Nurse — 36th evac and 71st evac

D iane volunteered, wanting to go where she was needed most. She gave up an assignment at VungTau, on the ocean, to go to Pleiku, near the Cambodian border. The incessant noise of incoming and outgoing fire, and an endless flow of patients from the jungle replaced ocean waves. New skills were gained, as feelings were lost.

"At first my senses were on overload; I cried every night. After awhile you had to turn your feelings off to avoid falling apart when you saw something devastating, and it was *all* devastating. These guys were only 18 and 19 years old! At some point I completely shut down, and was never able to cry at all until many years later at the Wall. It was a way to survive and do our job. We were the caretakers, and had to be positive and strong; lives depended on how brave, how smart, how quick and observant we were. My fear was if I broke down, someone's life could suffer or be lost because of it. We ran on adrenaline, spread so thin it created a super-human demand. But it took me years to realize I carried guilt, that no matter what we did, it wasn't enough. When you're so close to death, it's a part of life, and you don't fear your own death. The fear was not being able to save these young men, having a patient die on your shift."

Twenty-four hours after her last shift, Diane was greeted with hostility as she stepped off the plane in Minnesota. She'd been warned not to wear her uniform home, but had nothing else; another GI defended her, and ended up in a fist fight with the heckler.

"That was our welcome home after giving up a year of our lives. I was glad my parents were late, so they didn't have to witness that. Our country did much more than abandon us; it was open hostility. It was a confusing and angry time for me."

She worked in a civilian hospital for a few months, but found her sympathy for routine illness and surgeries lacking, and the skills learned in Vietnam of no use.

"I wasn't allowed to *do* those things here, I didn't fit in. And I saw how much I'd shut down when a female patient was watching this awful stuff from Cambodia and Vietnam on TV, sobbing at how devastating it was. I just stood there, no emotion, no tears. My mind knew it was sad and had compassion. My heart couldn't feel anything."

She worked at an Army hospital as a civilian for awhile, then re-upped, and went to Ft. Sam Houston. She was glad to be with people who understood her experience, and gratified to be helping Vietnam vets as they returned to 'the world'.

"It felt good to be with my peers again. We came home alone, totally segregated from those we'd served with, ended up at our parents' dining room tables for dinner that night, and pretended it was all behind us. But all I left behind was a part of me"

Diane met her husband at Ft. Sam, and left the Army in 1972 after her first child was born. She says she was on auto pilot for many years, being mom, wife and nurse, but not really feeling. In 1982, old emotions were stirred when she heard there'd be a dedication of a Vietnam Memorial Wall in Washington D.C. And it had names on it.

"I had to go, even though I could only remember one name. I couldn't deal with it all at once, so the memories of Vietnam seemed to come out one by one. I only remembered Eddie's name, and when I touched his name on the Wall, I started crying and I couldn't stop. The grief just poured out, and I had Eddie's funeral in my mind, all those years later. In Vietnam we never got to have funerals, so we never had a chance to go through that grief. But once I grieved for Eddie, there was another face; they just came one by one. Sometimes I couldn't see the face at first, but I could see the wound, and then I put the wound with a person. Then

I was able to grieve for each one of them, for his suffering, and for my own suffering too. Every time someone died, or was taken somewhere and I never knew what happened to them, a little piece of me went with them. What I lost in Vietnam was all those pieces of me. I couldn't get that back until I let myself remember, and grieve for them. My healing began at the Wall when I found that place in me that was closed and dead for so long."

Returning home, Diane was surprised to learn of controversy about the Wall, and that there would now be a statue of three men added to the memorial.

"I felt the Wall was perfect as it was, but if we were going to have a statue of the men, it became incomplete if we didn't have one for the women too. Something just stirred in me that this was the right thing to do, helping people realize the contribution women made there. It made me angry when so many said it would never work, but anger can be constructive. I was so sure this was the right thing to do, it made me fight harder. It was a high price to pay, but I believed in it so strongly, I quit my job and gave up everything but my husband and kids to make it a reality. My kids were only 4, 6, 8, and 10, and my Mom said she'd come and take care of them when I had to travel. I was so naive. I had no idea what I was opening myself up to. If I'd known it'd take 10 years and be as difficult as it was, I don't know if I would've attempted it, but I'm glad I did."

Suddenly, the memories she'd kept so closed and guarded, refusing to speak of them for 12 years, became public topics. This very private person was in the spotlight.

"Things were buried so deep, they were hard to see, much less describe. At first I only talked about where I was and what I did, but people wanted to know who I was, and why I was doing this. My motives and even my character were questioned. In a way it was good; I was forced to reach down and face my deeper feelings and fears. It made me feel even more that people needed to know women served and died in Vietnam too, and we all needed a way to heal. My work for the Womens Memorial was therapeutic, doing something positive for my sister and brother vets, after all those years they were misunderstood and maligned. It felt good to help people understand who Vietnam vets are. One of the greatest benefits for me with the project was finding women I'd served with, and bonding with them again. We lost touch for so many years because it was just too painful then. We were reminders to each other of the realities of war."

I know the painful memories will never go away, so I have to find a way to deal with them. And I don't think any veteran who was in Vietnam ever gets over the hyper-vigilance. Sometimes if you hear a sudden noise or a helicopter, it catches you off guard, and you have to find a way to bring yourself back to reality. The positive is, Vietnam set me on a course I never would've taken, and made me an advocate for women and for veterans. I think when you start to heal from it, you want to reach out and help others heal too. This memorial was my way of helping myself and others to heal.

Diane continues her mission of healing by speaking to schools and other groups. When I was photographing her, a group of children and adults arrived at the Women's Memorial. Little boys stuck fingers up the kneeling figure's nose, and Diane cringed silently. Then two girls sat down and began stroking the hand and shoulder of the same figure, talking in hushed tones, seeming to try to comfort her. Diane watched for a moment, then went over and began talking to them about what the Memorial represented, and what women did in Vietnam. They asked questions, entranced with this woman from history. Soon she had a crowd around her, and she brought those figures to life for them. When they were leaving, the girls wanted hugs, and the adults wanted her card, so they could get the book that tells more about the women and the memo-

rial. After they left, she sat down on the sandbags and put her hand on the knee of the woman the girls had been comforting. As she gazed at the anguished woman's face, her own expression changed. She spoke of how real these people are to her. She said when she came once in the winter, and there was snow on the memorial, she flashed back to how intense the heat was in Vietnam, and thought "Oh, they must be so cold." There is a piece of her heart in that memorial, in the anguished face of that nurse, still in that hospital in Vietnam. Her poem reveals this.

LEFT BEHIND — 1984

I search my soul
And memories of war
To find that lost space
That part of me that's gone
Left in Vietnam so many
Years ago and hoping
Someday to find it and
Make me whole again
I didn't leave behind
A limb, an arm or a leg
What is it then that's gone
It can't be seen and
Perhaps just as a lost
Limb it can never be
Retrieved

CORBIN CHERRY

1968-69 — 28 years old — 101st Airborne Chaplain

Corbin was 28, older than most of the boys in Vietnam. He had already completed school and been a minister four years, He speaks softly and slowly, with a hint of North Carolina drawl, as he remembers his 11 1/2 months as chaplain there, sleeping in the jungle with his troops all but five nights.

"We were at a firebase in the A Shau Valley, almost to the border of North Vietnam. I went to Vietnam with a mentality of healing, not of killing, so my mission was different than most. But I learned quickly that you just have to do whatever you can to survive, both physically and spiritually. I had to go and relieve another chaplain once, when he was unable to survive the loss of many of his troops in an ambush. I knew that could just as easily have been me. Everybody has a limit to how much they can take, and it was easy to see how many of us were pushed way beyond that limit."

Just two weeks before his tour was up, they were in a firefight.

"I crawled up a hill to get someone who'd been wounded, then ran down, carrying him. I stepped on a land mine, right where I'd just crawled, and got blown into a canyon. I knew immediately I would lose my leg."

Corbin healed physically, and found his emotional renewal through the time he spent alone in a remote cabin in North Carolina, writing a book of poetry on his experience in Vietnam, called "From Thunder To Sunrise"

"I had to be alone to truly come back from Vietnam. I had to figure out what to do with all the feelings and the memories that were troubling me. So I cried, I walked, I wrote, and I found my peace, and my healing. It was the best thing I could do for myself, and to honor the other men I served with."

Though he speaks of the experience with deep emotion and heartfelt tears, he also sees a positive side.

"It has never bothered me to share tears, any more than sharing words. Vietnam was a completely useless war, but now we have to move beyond that and take care of those who came back with physical and emotional wounds. Although I wish the war, and the killing, had never happened, it was the most incredible ministry months I've ever had. It was rewarding to realize I was there to bring comfort, not destruction, and that I had a great capability to do that."

He continues bringing healing to veterans as a chaplain in the VA hospital in San Francisco.

"After my experience in Vietnam, and losing my leg, my life and my work took a much deeper direction...I'm a very fortunate man. I wouldn't want to trade places with anyone."

Corbin skis, golfs, and does almost everything he did before he lost his leg. His love of writing continues, with a book on golf already completed, and one dealing with emotions nearly done. One of Corbin's poems, titled "I Knew You'd Be There" is reprinted in this book. It recalls the last moments of a boy Corbin comforted as he died.

This poem, written by Chaplain Corbin Cherry after his return from Vietnam, addresses one of the biggest fears veterans had, dying alone. It is a solemn reminder of over 58,000 young lives lost there, and of the daily reality that the men and women who served in Vietnam endured. The experience forever changed Corbin's life, and the lives of everyone who served there.

I KNEW YOU WOULD BE THERE

The day was aglow with the new sunlight,
but the air was filled with the sounds
of gunfire and human expressions of pain and fear.

From place to place I ran,
with more than I could understand to do,
and there all about me was the reality of this war.

"Over here, " some cried out,
and there in the midst of his day of dying,
was still another young face.

Someone who would never see his Mother again,
he would never again fish with his Dad,
and he would never walk down the lane with Mary or Sue.

I reached down to his lifeless body,
and under his head I placed my hand.
I could feel the warmth of his blood between my fingers.

As I prayed in that moment for God to intervene,
my prayer was interrupted by a voice
from his limp and lifeless body.

I looked at his face and there was a slight smile,
"I knew you would be here," he said.
"Thanks," and once again and for the last time, he lay limp.

My eyes filled with tears then and now,
to think that I was placed in such a sacred place
to be with Richard when he last breathed.

In a place so far away from everything that he loved,
there he died away from everyone,
except a friend who he trusted to come to him.

"I knew you would be here,"
the words ring over and over in my mind.
and when I think these weeks later about that time,
I realize I was given a perfect gift.

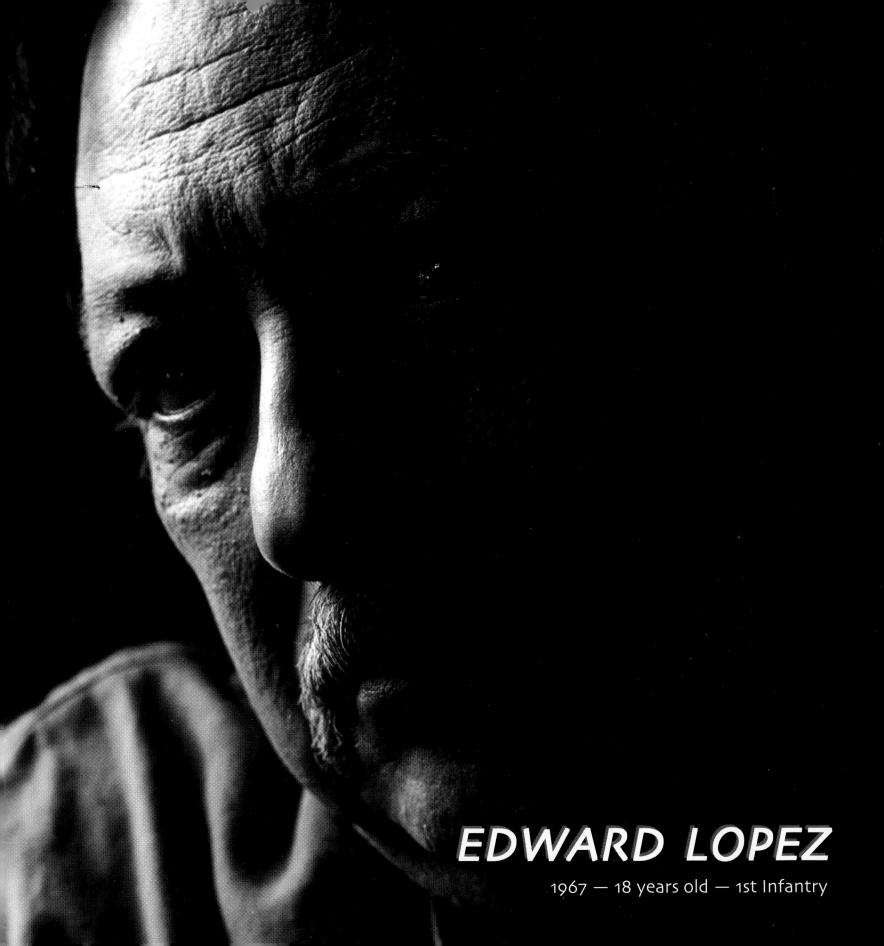

EDWARD LOPEZ

1967 — 18 years old — 1st Infantry

When Ed was drafted, he volunteered for office duty, hoping to avoid combat. But when he arrived in Vietnam, they drove into the jungle, to the Big Red "1".

"I knew I was in trouble. I ended up going on jungle patrol half of the time, and then when I came back in, my job was to handle the records of the dead in graves registration. It was pretty bad, 'cause I'd see stuff happen out there, and then have to live it all over again when I came back in."

While on jungle patrol, Ed was attacked by a Viet Cong.

"He was on top of me, face to face, his hands on my throat, and I couldn't breathe, I couldn't move. I knew I was going to die."

Then Ed heard a deafening shot, and his face was covered with blood. His enemy lay dead on top of him, and Ed's buddy stood next to him. That moment of near-death changed the way Ed related to life.

"You're always in a survival mode, always in fear. You can't compromise, or let yourself feel anything, except anger. We were dumped back into the world so fast, there was no chance to adjust. Right before I left, this VC broke through fire into our compound, firing his machine gun at us, while he was on fire, and I almost died again. Three days later, I get off the bus in Oakland, and a guy spits in my face. I wanted to kill him, and just three days ago, It would've been OK to do that. I'm glad he wasn't Asian, 'cause he'd be dead, and I'd be in prison. You don't just smile and go on, you don't just forget things like that. After I came home, I couldn't shake it, I just couldn't feel anymore."

Memories of Vietnam continued to haunt Ed. His internal war seemed to play itself out in his relationship with his wife.

"I became a wife beater. I'd say, 'Get outta my face, or I'll whack you'. She'd say if I loved her I wouldn't hit her. I just couldn't stand to have anyone in my face, and I think it was because of the experience I had over there. When I turned off my feelings in Vietnam to survive, they never came back. I couldn't let her in. I didn't know how to love another person."

"So I drank and did drugs. You drink so you don't see the guy's blood all over you, or see the guy on fire. I wanted it all to go away. I guess I drank because I didn't want to feel the pain anymore."

His wife left him, so he drank more, finally crashing his car, and winding up in jail. Fearing he might lose his kids too, he ultimately sought help from his best friend, another Vietnam vet, to quit drugs and drinking.

"I just graduated from photography school. Other than getting sober, it's the first good thing I've done for myself...the first thing I've completed. I'm proud of that."

"I've never told anybody any of this before, except my buddy from Vietnam. It's a dark side of me that I don't let anyone into. I got lost for 30 years. I can't do anything about the past, but I can try to live a good life from this day on. I just want to let that wound heal, and be human again, maybe have another chance to love somebody."

Ed said he was wound up for three days after our interview, but then found it to be a very healing experience. Ed is now in his 14th year of sobriety, works full time, and has just started a photography business with a friend.

TIM O'BRIEN

1969 — 22 years old — Infantry — Americal Division, My Lai

*T*im was opposed to the war, and had serious thoughts of desertion.

"I went feeling a mixture of terror, guilt, and anger at God for making a war and making me have to be in it. Coming home, I was radically changed, divided, not whole anymore. I was happy to be alive, but filled with doubt, self-recrimination, and guilt, for what I had been a part of there, and for not having the courage to say no. I had a plan to desert when I was in Seattle in advanced training, and I'll always regret not doing it. It was the right thing for me to do, and I thought I was the kind of guy to do the right thing, but it was hard to walk away. I had this terror of people thinking badly of me for running away from war, of embarrassing my family and my hometown, of being thought of as a coward, never being able to live in my country again."

For Tim, it was harder to go to Canada than to go to Vietnam.

"I admire the courage of those who went, risking their family's shame and anger, people thinking badly of them, all the consequences of exile. You never know if you're doing it for reasons of conscience, or if you're just afraid to die. It takes guts to say no. If you go with the system, people clap your back and say you're doing the right thing, your country loves you, blah blah blah. You get all that emotional support, you don't get for going to Canada. War was what I expected; terrible, dangerous and gruesome. You could feel the insanity and evil. But what still haunts me is making that decision, feeling like I was going crazy. That's the nightmare for me. I dream about Vietnam every few months, but I dream a lot more about that. It's made me a total insomniac; I wake up maybe 30 times a night."

Before Vietnam Tim's aspirations included joining the State Department

"Afterwards, I had no life plan because my value system and my personality had changed. I was full of self-doubt, where before Vietnam I was very on track, the Phi Beta Kappa type; I knew I was going to succeed. Before Vietnam, I got a fellowship to go to grad school in Government at Harvard, so when I came back, I just did that because it was something to do. I only talked to a few close friends about Vietnam, so most people didn't even know I was there."

His first novel was published in 1973, while he was still at Harvard.

"I was silent about the war, but I began writing about it; I spoke through my writing. I wasn't an English major, and I wasn't planning on becoming a writer. But the human capacity is to try to salvage some good out of something very bad. For me, the good was re-examining myself and becoming a writer. "

"But I feel like I'm trapped by my life. Every book I write has something to do with Vietnam, even if it's not about Vietnam. I'll always return to it. It affected my life so completely, in hundreds of little ways we never think about. Like smoking. I started there because they gave us free cigarettes, and I thought I was going to die anyway. How could smoking be dangerous when I was getting shot at? It's another daily reminder of that one year of my life."

The depression, guilt, and shame he felt then, never quite goes away

"Vietnam happened when I was young and scared, when relationships and trust and other things are formed, so it shapes you into a certain kind of person. It seeps into your blood and your cellular tissue, and forms who you are, so it's always with you. It's a lot like having cancer, losing a parent, or getting divorced. They're traumatic things you'll always be troubled about and think about. In your dream life they come back to revisit you. "

"War is a thing you'll never forget, when you almost get killed every day. We can't erase the past, we just have to live with it. I just tried to salvage something from the wreckage and deal with trauma the way everybody has to... It's either that or go insane."

Tim's writing began when he sent his accounts of war home to Minnesota newspapers. He is now a best-selling, award-winning author, and knows "War stories aren't always about war...they're about the human heart."

MAX CLELAND

1967-68 — 24 years old — Army, 1st Air Cavalry

*M*ax greets me from an overstuffed chair with big smile and outstretched hand. He asks where I want him, then decides he should be at his desk. With one fluid movement, his left arm grabs the wheel chair, his body arcs through the air, and he's in the driver's seat, moving quickly across the office. Then he repeats the ballet, and is in his desk chair before I can pick up my cameras and follow him. His desk is covered with biblical and motivational passages, words he lives by, words he needs. "IF IT IS TO BE, IT IS UP TO ME" jumps off the corner of the desk; that is how Max lives. His faith is what helps him put one foot in front of the other. But he has no feet. And no legs. And no right arm. He is not a religious zealot; he's a man who refuses to let what he doesn't have get in the way of who he is and what he does. He can swim, drive a car, play basketball, and dance in his wheelchair. And he is a United States Senator.

Max had to fight depression and anger after being wounded, but he knew from the beginning that he was not going to let his injuries get in his way. He knew it even when doctors told a friend who visited in the hospital, "If he gets up in the morning and puts his shirt on, it will tire him for the whole day." Now he follows a three-hour exercise, meditation, and prayer regime each morning that wears me out to hear about it, but it's his insurance against living down to the expectations of that doctor. Fatigue be damned, this is his daily declaration that Max Cleland is alive and well, and as long as he has one thumb left to make the Thumbs Up sign, it will be so.

"You know, when you're down to one thumb, you gotta use it! Somebody told me I was so positive, they gave me a brass thumbs up for my desk. Now it's kind of my trademark. I had glass ones made for the Max Cleland Alive Day Awards."

Max used to try to ignore the anniversary of that day in Vietnam. But he could never turn off the tape that plays in his mind: he gets out of the chopper, looks back as it lifts off, spots the grenade on the ground, thinks he must have dropped it and reaches out with his right arm to pick it up. Seconds later, the young 6'2" captain is lying on the ground, both legs and right arm blown to shreds, fighting to stay alive. Now every April 8, he celebrates winning that fight, an idea given to him by his friend Jim Mayer.

"Jim celebrated the day he lost both legs in Vietnam; it's the day he got to live. Isn't that a great way to think of it? So I began celebrating my own Alive Day, and then created the Max Cleland Alive Day Award in 1999 and had a party with prizes! Each year on that date, we'll give the award to someone who helped somebody stay alive. We presented the first one to David Lloyd, who was first to me on the battlefield, and helped save my life. This year we'll honor a helicopter crew (the pilot is a Vietnam vet) that did an amazing air rescue to save the life of a man in a burning building in Atlanta. Now it's a day I look forward to. It's all in how you look at it."

For 31 years Max believed he'd maimed himself with his own grenade. Medals offered for his careless act embarrassed him. Then in 1999, David Lloyd saw Max on a TV show about medics; he called Max and said he was there, and knew the real story.

"When Dave told me he cut off my uniform for a tourniquet, I knew he was really there. Then he said 'It wasn't your grenade, the guy behind you dropped it'. It was unbelievable! When Dave got to him after he'd helped me, the guy was crying, saying 'It was my grenade! It's my fault!' He'd only been in-country a couple of days, and someone told him if you straighten the pins on your grenades, it's easier to pull out in combat, so he did that to all his grenades. He was a walking bomb. He was punctured with schrapnel, but didn't lose any limbs. So I got blown up, and he didn't. But it was just an accident of war. I'm just relieved to know I didn't do this to myself"

No anger for the man who changed his life and his body; only relief. Did his strength come from believing he'd created it, so he had to find a way to overcome it?

"Living was a more difficult choice for me than dying. Everything was a battle, but I had to fight, I had to have something to feel good about. The war never stopped for me in many ways. In Vietnam it was a battle to survive, then the battle was the hospitals and rehab, and surviving outside the hospital. I mean, if I couldn't fight back and win a life of independence and earn a living, drive to work, those kind of things, what was I gonna do? When I got out of the hospital, I went back to Georgia, and I was unemployed, living in my parents' house, no job, no car, no girlfriend, no hope, no future. So what the heck, I ran for the State Senate in 1970, and amazingly enough, won. I was 28, the youngest senator and the only Vietnam vet at that time."

Max felt called to serve his country since spending a college semester in D.C. in 1963. That's why he volunteered for Vietnam. After the war he feared he'd never realize his dream of entering politics, but his courage and determination won out. He went on to become state Secretary of State, administrator of the VA, and finally US Senator. But a period of unemployment in 1974 threw him into a deep depression.

"Then in 1975, pursuing a job at the VA, I got in my battered Olds, and set out to drive from Georgia to D.C. Somewhere on I-95, I reached out, and God answered."

Max reviewed the things he'd accomplished against huge odds, and wondered why he still felt empty and sad. He'd been so determined to do it all on his own, with no help from God or anyone else. But he felt so alone. As his tears merged into the rain on the windshield he cried, "God forgive me! God help me!", and finally felt at peace. He found a meaning in his life, a reason to be alive, outside his job. Realizing that he needed help and inspiration seems to have led him to want to inspire others.

"Everyone needs inspiration, whether it's quotes or people or stories or seeing courageous lives. We all need inspiration and motivation to live. I was invited to be on the Larry King show last year and I was scared to death, but it was a great thing. A lady from the midwest called, and had checked into a motel, unbeknownst to her kids and husband, to commit suicide. She was disabled and felt like she was a drain on her family. She turned on the TV in the motel, and there we were. She was inspired by my story and went home and got counseling. I got a very touching card from her kids last Christmas. We all need inspiration to go on sometimes."

Inspiration and people are like oxygen to Max. They give him life. He inhales them, and that allows him to keep going, and to keep giving to others the hope and the Max-isms they need.   Every day, and every night, and throughout his two books, Max shares with people the life force that has sustained him for all these years.

"I love politics and public service because I believe we can generate hope in people. Vietnam marred this country and the generation that fought it, for a long time. It's one of those things you don't ever get over; life is never the same, whether you were physically wounded or not. But you carry on and do the best with what you've got. It took me a long time to find the strength I needed, to make some sense of all the tragedy, and find meaning in my life. A favorite saying is, 'Turn your scars into stars'. I know dreams can come true if you really believe in them, and never give up. I know that because...this is my dream job."

I'd interviewed dozens of vets before Max; many were wounded, but none had lost three limbs. Reading about him before I went, I got a sense of his positive attitude, but not of his physical presence. It's amazing how his attitude overcomes his missing parts, not just for him, but for everyone around him. After a few minutes, I no longer noticed what was missing. All I could do was try to keep up with the constant motion of his mind punctuated by his left hand, his animation, his clear-eyed smile. His body is only 4' tall, but his presence is still 6'2".

"This poem says better than I ever could, how I feel about my life."

A SOLDIER'S PRAYER
– by an unknown confederate soldier

I asked God for strength, that I might achieve;
I was made weak, that I might learn humbly to obey.
I asked for health, that I might do greater things;
I was given infirmity, that I might do better things.
I asked for riches, that I might be happy;
I was given poverty, that I might be wise.
I asked for power, that I might have the praise of men.
I was given weakness, that I might feel the need of God.
I asked for all things, that I might enjoy life;
I was given life, that I might enjoy all things.
I got nothing that I asked for — but everything I had hoped for.
Almost despite myself, my unspoken prayers were answered.
I am among all men, most richly blessed.

ROBERT SHEA

1966-68 — 26 years old — Civilian Advisor for MACV

*B*ob was out of the service, and working on his master's degree in psychology, when he got an offer to go to Vietnam as a civilian.

"They said I'd be helping refugees, but it quickly turned into things like training Kit Carson Scouts and provincial soldiers. But I believed that JFK, kill a commie for Christ thing, and I felt like we were helping them. I really liked working with the Vietnamese people, as well as with other professional people, mostly retired green beanies, who couldn't make it back in the States."

He got hit by an RPG, and nearly lost his arm. He was in the Naval hospital for almost 10 months before he could return to grad school and work

"My homecoming was easier, since I was in the hospital, and had time to talk about what happened. I now find in my counseling practice, that the ones who were wounded do much better, having that transition. In WWII, guys came back together on a ship, so they had all that time to talk about it, laugh and cry about it. That's what we did in the hospital, and it was very healthy. Many of my clients who weren't wounded, have severe PTSD. Some have said, 'I wish I had your arm, I wish I had scars I could show people. My scars are all inside, and no one can see them.' "

Bob has a Ph.D. in psychology, and finds one of the rewards of Vietnam is being able to help other veterans in his practice.

"Vietnam gave me a direction in my work. More than half my clients are Vietnam vets who have PTSD, and I get many of the hard-core cases from the vet center. I've also been on the other side of the desk, getting therapy for PTSD myself. I had survivors guilt, hyper-alertness, and I didn't want to get close to anyone because they die. I measure friends by whether I'd share a fox-hole with them, carrying the survival mode with me. I'm forced to deal with my issues constantly, through my clients, so it's therapeutic for me.

"Vietnam will always be a part of us, so the object of therapy is not to forget, but just to remember and not feel the same emotional pain. I tell clients the definition of PTSD is 'a normal reaction to an abnormal situation,' so that makes them feel normal, not crazy. Many later tell me that is what helped them most. I was the first person to tell them they weren't crazy."

"But I can't deny the effects. I was very outgoing before Vietnam, but I'm reclusive, and don't have many real friends now. I became estranged from my family, too. My aunt wouldn't even let my cousin, who I was very close to, visit me in the hospital; they thought I'd be a bad influence. Vietnam was undoubtedly the most emotional, physical, intellectual, and spiritual thing I've ever done in my life."

"What I'd like to say to the people who read this book is, 'It's still not too late to say thanks.' I can't think of any of my clients who had a good homecoming. They were punished for talking about it, punished for being there. They didn't get thanks for risking their lives. They felt like outcasts, and many still do."

Bob wept many times, folded his arms, hung his head, wiggled his legs and feet, his emotion evident in his body language. Bob continues to help other Vietnam veterans heal, offering psychological counseling through his practice.

LILY ADAMS

1969-70 — 21 years old — Triage Nurse

*L*ily was a pacifist, and did not want to go, but contrary to belief, not all nurses were volunteers in Vietnam.

"I was in ICU with amputees and severe wounds, and I got so attached to patients, who were mostly my age or younger; they were peers, little brothers. I had to get out, so I volunteered for Triage, but I got attached even in the few minutes I had with them; they'd share intimate details about their lives and families, precious memories they want to share before they die. Then they die; as quickly as they enter your life they leave, and the loss is so painful. I was like a robot by the end of my tour. I totally locked my heart; I didn't want to be hurt anymore, and I didn't know how to help them die. I had a guy with all four limbs gone, begging me to kill him, and watched a corpsman take him away, not knowing what happened to him. I felt so helpless. Then someone wants to tell me there's justification for that war? I don't think so. "

"Vietnam was the best and the worst experience I ever had in nursing. But when I came home, I couldn't focus or absorb new things, I'd get very depressed and angry and not know why. But the 'why' is, I saw innocent human beings, taught by the government to kill, to disassociate from their heart to do what they had to, filled with anger and hate when a buddy got killed next to them. I carried all this around for years, and never knew about PTSD."

Now Lily has learned a great deal about Post Traumatic Stress Disorder.

PTSD isn't a Vietnam problem. Other wars had it, accident or rape victims have it, many people do. How could you *not* have PTSD after being surrounded by death every day for a year? And if it's not dealt with, it goes to the next generation. Look at children of the holocaust or African Americans, still reacting from the PTSD of ancestors. We were put in a box, but we can educate people that we don't all fit that stereotype. I'm a woman, I'm not on the street, I have a home, a job, a family, I'm not on drugs. But I also have PTSD that's not going to go away. I'm an Agent Orange victim, I've got everything that came out of Vietnam, including birth defects, health problems, and the kind of attitudes Vietnam vets have."

Her first pregnancy ended at 7 1/2 months, when she almost died of eclampsia.

"My twins didn't make it. I went into a deep depression and saw what a loss that is, for a woman who had a son in a war. It was so hard for me to lose babies in my womb, and I became painfully aware of what it must be like to lose a son after 18 or 19 years, for economics. As a result, I didn't want to be in nursing anymore; it brought back Vietnam. I went back to school, and gave up my identity as a nurse and healer, which is who I am. "

While she was in school, Lily was pregnant with her daughter, and denied it for 8 months. Four years later, with her son, she did the same thing, still afraid of being hurt again.

"So another woman and I started a group called HAND (helping after neo-natal death). By then I had my psychology degree, so I counseled parents who had lost babies. Through that, I got into counseling at the Vet Center, and I did that for eight years. I quit last year to do a research study for the VA on Asian American vets who had race-related experiences in Vietnam. This taught me I need to be a healer, not a researcher. I feel like I'm without oxygen right now, not doing this work. So I'm starting a practice, working with Vietnam vets, and other people who've experienced trauma. Vets are a part of me, I miss them. I guess I have to re-live the war on a regular basis, though I don't want to, because I don't want to forget it, and don't

want others to forget it. It's my way to honor the dead. I don't know their names, but their spirit is here. I use that to educate."

Going to the Wall in 1983 was the beginning of a long road to healing.

"It was the dedication, so I was with thousands of other vets. They came up and thanked me for being there, and told me stories about experiences with other nurses. For the first time I was being recognized for what I did in Vietnam by people who mattered to me: other Vietnam vets. Other than my family and a few close friends, they matter more to me than anyone. And I matter to them. When I go to the Wall now, I get very angry, then I get very sad for all the loss. There are 11 panels from when I was there, and my dead are on them. But I only remember one name because I've tried to forget."

"It was dark, and I thought I'd never find him. Then I just rubbed my hand along the wall from one end to the other, and by the time I got to the other end, I was hysterical. I hurt for ALL of them, I felt I took care of all of them. It was the first time I really got the grief out. "

"My mom has told me, 'You're not Lily'. When I first got home, we hugged, and I didn't feel anything; that's a very unusual experience. I was numb, emotionally dead. We had to numb ourselves for protection, and I just couldn't get it back. There were many times I went numb with my husband and children, and felt like my soul had left me. I would have to hug them just to try to get my soul back. That feeling of loss is the same as I felt when men died in Vietnam. The other thing I think happened as a result of Vietnam is that I'm not usually a happy person. I shocked myself once when I laughed at my son, a real belly laugh, and realized I hadn't had a belly laugh in years. I have to work hard at being happy, but I'm never happy like I was before Vietnam. I'm very intense. I've seen man's inhumanity to man, and that has a great effect on you. I work at it, but I'm not a happy person anymore."

"Vietnam veterans are no different than any other vets, and we deserve respect. We were injured twice — once in Vietnam, and again when we came home. For years, nobody even knew we existed, nobody talked about it. We could've all died there, and nobody would've known the difference. It was like in families of abuse, there was a conspiracy of silence, where nobody says anything. Nobody defended us, even the military organizations. So we started the Vietnam Veterans of America, so we can defend ourselves, and educate people, especially people that could make a difference, like the media. No one stood up for us, so we had to stand up for ourselves. The Vietnam Memorial was something we had to create, and we had to create our Welcome Home. Perhaps someday we can get that support from our peers."

Lily has a private practice, counseling vets and others with PTSD. She recently had an Agent orange exam, and found that she has fibromyalgia, related to her exposure. Her son's birth defect and the loss of her twins are also thought to be related.

The poems on the following page, written by Lily after her return, reflect the feelings of many nurses.

Being a Vet is Like Losing a Baby — 1981

Being a vet
Is like
Losing a baby

No one says
Anything to you
And you don't
Say anything to them.

The Friendship Only
Lasted a Few Seconds

He said "Mom"
And I responded
And became her.
I never lied to him
And I couldn't
Explain that to others.
I got all and more back,
But the friendship
Only lasted a few seconds.

And he called me Mary.
I wished she could
Be there for him.
I felt I was in
Second place,
But I did the
Best I could.
And the friendship
Only lasted a few seconds.

And he told me,
"I don't believe this,
I'm dying for nothing."
Then he died.
Again, the friendship
Only lasted a few seconds.

How can the World
Understand any of this?
How can I keep the
World from forgetting?
After all, the friendship
Only lasted a few seconds.

JESSE NIGHTHAWK

18 years old — 173rd Airborne Brigade

"The government has been lying to my people for hundreds of years. I guess I shouldn't have been surprised they lied about Vietnam."

Jesse, like many others, went to the war feeling he was doing his patriotic duty, and found out quickly that it wasn't what we were led to believe. He returned a different person.

"I felt very alienated when I came home, and there was no deprogramming at all; your mind and body are still in combat. There was plenty of medication over there, alcohol and every kind of drug. If you were a social drinker when you went, the stress would push you over the edge into some kind of chemical dependency. I just kept doing it when I came back, maybe even more, 'cause I had more time, and didn't have to worry about getting shot. Then, within five years of coming home from Vietnam, I lost my older brother, and my Mom and Dad. I was going through all this trauma; the great unexplainable loss I felt after Vietnam, then all these other losses. It was eating at me so damn bad, I had to do something to make it go away, to forget about it; I just bottomed out. I got a DUI and ended up in jail with these hard criminals. I lost my job, and damn near lost my family. That's when I woke up and knew I had to start healing."

Jesse has since tried to turn the "worst experience of my life" into a positive motivation to help him focus on music, his true passion.

"I knew if I could make it through that, I should be able to do almost anything. When I finally got enough courage to visit the Wall, it gave me some measure of closure, some healing, and I was able to write about it. That was the hardest thing for me to do, but it was when I finally started healing."

Jesse is married, drives a truck, and writes and performs music all over the country. "APO San Francisco" is dedicated to the veterans whose names appear on the Vietnam Memorial Wall.

As I stood there at that wall
It looked so dark, so cold and tall
watching the families and friends
Trying hard to recall those days
They didn't seem that far away
But for them, it was a lifetime ago.

– (from *APO San Francisco* , by Jesse Nighthawk)

DUANE SKATES

18 years old — Marines

*D*uane's Dad was a Marine, so he always knew he'd follow that path.

"I enlisted after high school, and I didn't really mind going to Vietnam. I got shot a few times while I was over there, and it was no big deal. Just part of the job. The one at the end of my tour almost took me out though"

He woke up four months later in a hospital, with a Japanese nurse standing over him, and when he saw slanted eyes, he thought that he had been captured. He jumped up and punched her.

"I was trained to react quickly to survive, and didn't know where I was. We thought it'd be great to be back here in the 'World' (the U. S.) where it was safe. But we soon found out Nam was safer in some ways, where you at least knew who the enemy was. I really wanted to go back, to get even for what was done to me, but they wouldn't send me, no matter how much I tried to talk my way back there. I didn't like being here, it felt more threatening to be home. I felt like somebody had put an upside-down glass over me, and I was all alone in there, watching the world go by on the other side. I didn't belong anymore, I didn't fit. I'd aged so much over there."

Duane tried to adapt, using tactics he learned to survive in Vietnam

"One of the things they taught us is you stay alive by getting angry, getting the adrenaline going. You don't get too close to anybody, because they might die, and if you get emotional, you're a liability. So we come back to the states and try to get on with life, get married. Then he starts blowing off steam, and she doesn't know why. His mind says 'I did it before, and it saved my fanny, so this is what I should be doing'."

Duane has been married to the same woman four times, and divorced three. They have been separated again now for a year.

"One time she reached up to touch a scar *(from a Vietnam wound)* on my chest, and I grabbed her arm with one hand, moving to punch her with the other. I didn't see a hand coming toward me, I saw a bayonet. My wife said she never knew how I was going to react, and that's what scared her the most."

Duane works for the California Department of Veteran Services, helping veterans with their claims against the VA, and feels it has helped him deal with his own problems.

"This helps me work through my own stuff, but it also means it's always in my face, so it can cause a few problems. But it's the way I get to them. They wouldn't send me back, but now they have to pay, to deal with me at this level. If the veteran wins, I win...This is my new form of combat."

I sense a very controlled and well-directed anger still bubbling inside Duane as he speaks. He often makes statements in the third person when speaking of his own challenges, referring to problems of the general veteran population. He is the voice of the veteran, and enjoys helping them receive benefits they're entitled to.

Duane was recently promoted to an administrative position within the Veterans Service.

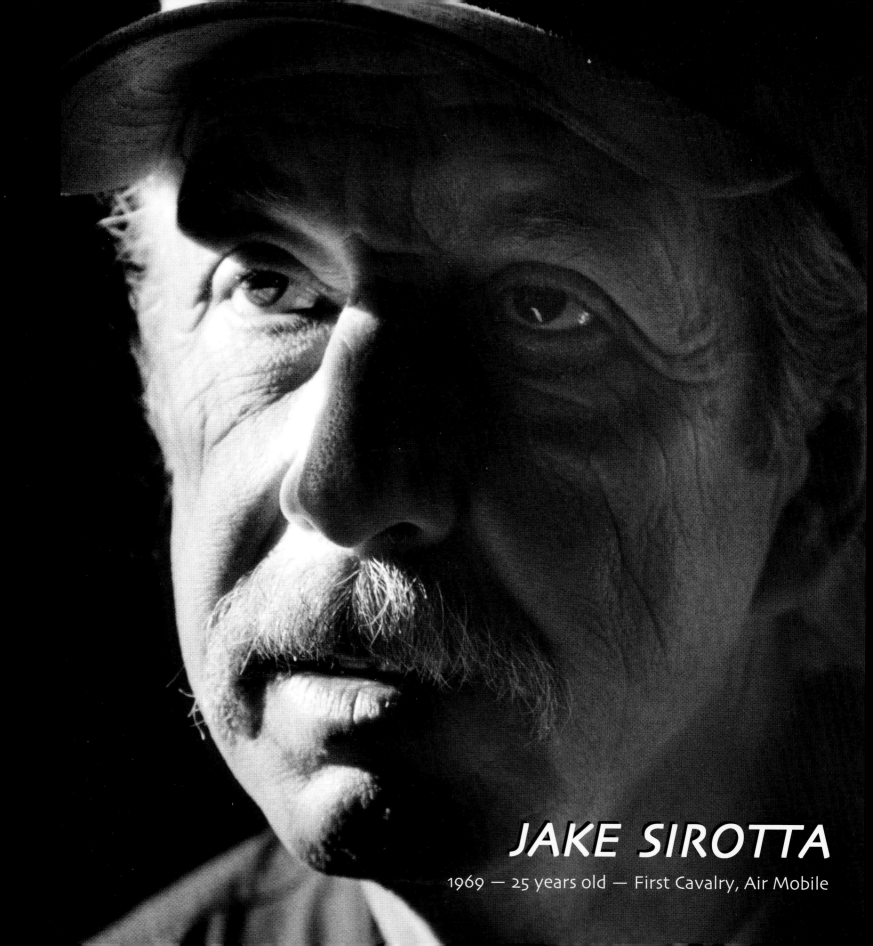

JAKE SIROTTA

1969 — 25 years old — First Cavalry, Air Mobile

I interviewed Jake at the bar where he runs a cold sandwich concession. He spends most of his time there, though he quit drinking years ago.

" I was drafted, but committed for four years so I could go to OCS. I went to Germany as a 2nd Lieutenant, and was a Captain by the time I got to Vietnam. My first night in the field, as company commander, we were attacked by a North Vietnamese regiment. We had a platoon right below us, and when we went down to rescue them we had 19 dead and 43 wounded. It was monsoon season, and the run-off on the hill was red. Blood."

He got a Silver Star that night, survived eight more months, came home, and was discharged the next day. Two days later he went back to work for Sylvania.

"They offered me a much bigger job than I had when I left, and I was really happy; it was a great promotion, with a car, expense account, and a big raise. I didn't realize it, but I just wasn't ready for it. I only lasted nine months, and I told my boss to f--- off. I went like that for years, job after job. I don't understand it, because that certainly wasn't me before I went. I've been able to stay here eight years, since I have no real boss. I barely get by, living at poverty level mostly. The best job I ever had was at Sylvania, but I just wasn't ready for it. It just didn't register that I should take time to decompress after what I'd been through. My family encouraged me to forget about what happened and get on with my life, and that's all I wanted to do. Well, you just don't forget something like that."

"It was fought mostly by 18 and 19 year olds; there were none of the old, professional soldiers where I was. The most stressful thing was having all these 18 year old kids under my command. They were somebody's kids, and if I did one thing wrong, I might get 15 or 20 of them killed. That's a heavy load to carry around every day and every night. I never slept, worrying about that. You try not to get close to anybody, but that's impossible. How can you be in that situation and not cling to friends? I still have flashbacks of that."

Jake never knew what PTSD was until he got into counseling.

"I was blown away; the definition was me. The intensity, the carnage, the chaos, it's beyond anyone's comprehension. That's why people still suffer from PTSD. It's a mystery, you can't really put your finger on it; you don't get sick, and there's not really a cure. I wish I'd never gone to Vietnam, even if it meant I had to go to Canada. It took away a piece of my life, it ruined the only relationship I cared about. At least she got me to quit drinking, though. I know it's not all Vietnam, but that was a huge part of it."

"When I was working on Jesse Jackson's campaign in 1988, he came here, and wanted to talk to a Vietnam vet. He asked me what I thought of the Memorial in D.C., and when I told him I hadn't seen it, he flew me there, put me up for three nights, and gave me $150 spending money, just so I could see it."

"It just took my breath away. All those names, the names of people who were with me. When I came over that hill and saw it, it just brought me to my knees, just dropped me right to the ground. There was the whole horrible nightmare, forever etched in stone."

JERRY AHLERING

Navy Officer

*J*erry had planned to be an attorney before he went to Vietnam. Instead, he ended up working his way through the system that sent him there, and became an administrator at the VA hospital in San Francisco. In 1997, he spoke to other Vietnam veterans at the dedication of a monument in their honor:

"...We all shared one common thread — We feared we would die, or we feared we would be called upon to kill. We simply feared, and we often still do. Mostly we wished we had not been so alone."

Jerry's Dad was pro-war, and he was too, until he got there; his siblings were totally against it. It separated their family, as it did our nation, and often turned friends against friends. Vietnam vets returned from war, alone, mentally and physically wounded, to a hostile environment in a nation divided.

"It was a very impersonal war; the enemy was often far away and faceless, so it's easy to kill. Women and children are no different than men—it's all killing, and its all wrong. It haunts for life—You recall its sights, you hear its sounds, you remember the smells that came with fear."

"Vietnam vets are people—friends and neighbors, who served their country...What makes us different, what makes us Vietnam vets, is something we understand, but we are afraid nobody else will."

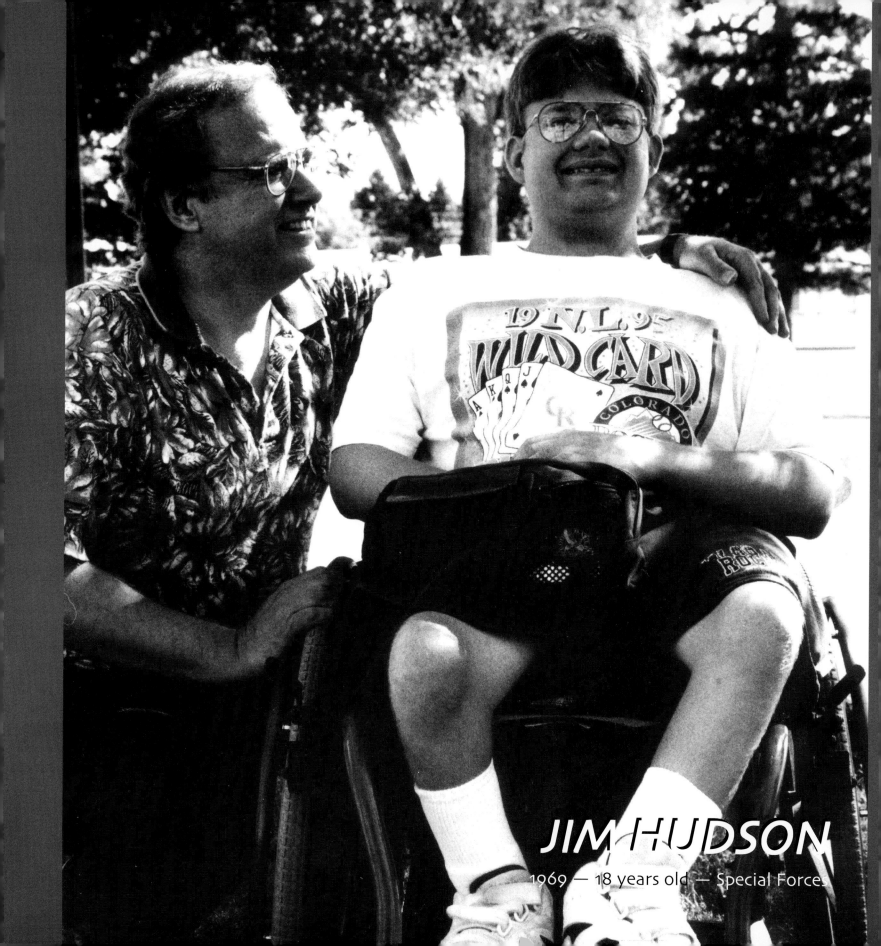

JIM HUDSON

1969 — 18 years old — Special Forces

"At 18, you don't have any concept of war, or its consequences, so I joined to have an adventure, get away from home. It was the worst year of my life. I got so I questioned and challenged everything, especially to do with the government. That's what got me into veterans affairs when I got home."

"I worked in the veterans service office while I was in college. When I graduated, I was the Disabled American Veterans lobbyist in Colorado for six years. So by the time my son Jeremy was born in 1979, I knew about Agent Orange, and the many ways it affects veterans.

Nobody knows if Agent Orange was the cause of Jeremy or any other child having Spina Bifida, but there's enough evidence, from several studies, that the VA has made it a service-connected disability for children of Vietnam Veterans.

"Disabilities vary, but Jeremy is paralyzed, doesn't have normal stature or development, his bladder and bowel don't work right, he has hydrocephalus so he has a shunt (tube to drain fluid from the brain), learning disabilities, and he's had 15 surgeries since he was born. To know that these are all things that MY problem of Agent Orange exposure may have caused for Jeremy, is very difficult."

Jim's wife Fran agrees, "We made a decision after Jeremy was born that we wouldn't have any more children. It was too much of a risk, knowing we might have another child with Spina Bifida. It was just so emotionally, physically, and financially draining, we just couldn't take that chance."

"Fran and I both worked in the area of disabilities before Jeremy was born, so we were able to stand up for his rights, and get things done. Jeremy has now become involved in working for rights of the disabled, and was instrumental in getting the first, front row wheelchair seats in the country, at the new Coors field. He also helped get mid-court seats at the new Pepsi Center. He sees his parents are advocacy-oriented, so he's decided if you don't like something, you work to get them to change it. He's got an attitude, but I think it's a good one. He has a lot of learning problems, he struggles, but he's had special education services, and still has them in junior college. But he's doing something he wants to do."

Jim feels spouses and children of veterans get overlooked, and it's important to him to work to ensure families get the help they need too.

"The VA is authorized only to serve veterans, and they often don't even do that very well. Vietnam changed the course of my life. I saw that people could literally be killed because a congressperson decides they don't mind risking someone else's life. And I saw the same congressperson turn away when vets and families needed help afterward. So it did make me angry, and I channeled that anger. But the anger and the survivor guilt also have a lot of internal affect on you, physically and psychologically."

"But in some ways I wouldn't have it any other way. If I hadn't gone to Vietnam, and didn't have this anger, and didn't have a child with Spina Bifida, I'd probably end up like some of my high school friends who didn't go, just working for some company selling widgets. To me this feels better, it feels like I've done something to make a difference in my life, and in my child's life, my family's life, my community's life. So I feel pretty good. I guess I'm just an optimist, and find the best in what life hands me. I've been very fortunate that I haven't had a lot of the problems that other guys had, with alcohol and drugs, and relationships."

Jim does consulting work with Veterans Families of America. Jeremy attends college classes and has a job at the new stadium, as an usher and a greeter.

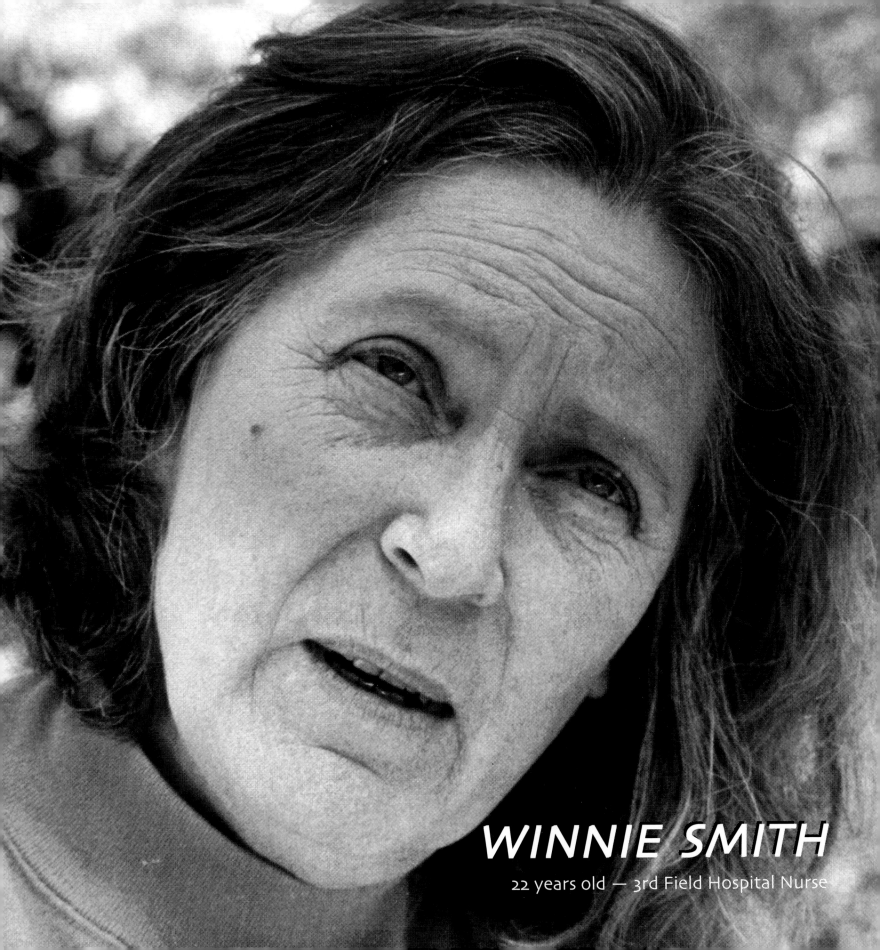

WINNIE SMITH

22 years old — 3rd Field Hospital Nurse

The week I interviewed Winnie, there was a tragic event at a high school, where two students killed several others, leaving the nation in shock.

"The media refers to the shooters as children, but they were 17 and 18, the same age as most guys in Vietnam. People are so aware of the impact this will have on the other kids for the rest of their lives, but there seems to be no awareness of what happens with guys in combat. They think, well you've served your country and that was good, now come home and get on with life, do everything you were going to do before you went. But war changes you."

"I saw changes in them after just a few months. They became so full of anger and despair, seeing buddies killed and other things. Imagine being 18, terrified, the enemy all around, machine gun in hand. You get in a situation, end up killing civilians, then come home and have to live with it the rest of your life. You can never tell anyone at home about it, because if they knew what you did, they could never accept you. You can't even accept it yourself."

One of the hardest things for nurses to accept was "expected casualties".

"We'd put them behind screens, and check on them every couple hours to see if they were still alive. These were 18, 19 year old guys, 10,000 miles from home, with no one to talk to, just laying there alone, waiting to die. And there were times I was in a hurry for them to die, because I needed the respirator for someone who was going to live. And what that does to your heart...It changes your *soul*, it makes you hard. Over there we all had to do it, so it seemed OK, but after you come back you know you can never tell anyone; if they knew, they could never love me. And I think deep down, I still feel no one could ever love me, because I've seen that part of myself I find so ugly. Which I think is why I never married."

Winnie stuffed it all, never let herself read or think about Vietnam.

"But in 1983 my cousin sent me the book "Home Before Morning". On the first page was a description of an expected casualty, and I was suddenly crying so hard I couldn't breathe. I stopped answering the phone, didn't go back to work and didn't call anybody. I'd just hide in the house with the lights off and cry, feeling like I was going crazy, not knowing what else to do. I was so scared, I thought they were probably going to institutionalize me, so I was afraid to let anybody see me. It seemed my life had suddenly been reduced to nothing, and I couldn't even function in the nothingness."

"My book began as a way to get it all out. I had dreams and flashbacks, so I'd write it down to help make it go away. It was like a virtual ride – I was more there than I was here. I grew up in a patriotic family, with great respect for what it meant to serve your country. But my family didn't want to know what happened to me, so they never read the book. But it helped me forgive myself for who I was when I was over there. I got past the first rush of pain, but I don't think I'll ever regain what I had, or who I was, before I went."

"I can't do nursing anymore. I've gone from being emotionally dead to painfully alive, and I have to try to temper that. It wasn't just the killing, it was the total loss of a belief system. I went there with dreams of helping, but I lost my dreams, my innocence, the sense of fellow Americans as being good people, of me being a good person, and of my government being good. So that left God I guess...and I knew if there was a God that place couldn't exist."

"If people understood the depth to which you're changed in war, they would not be so quick to support it. And if they back the government in sending us to war, we shouldn't have to beg for help when we come home."

Winnie's book, AN AMERICAN DAUGHTER GOES TO WAR, details her experiences in Vietnam.

GEORGE GIBBS

1970 — 25 years old — Army Recon Scout and Right Gunner

G eorge was a newlywed when he got drafted. He was only in Vietnam for two months when he was hit by a rocket-propelled grenade (RPG).

"Usually if a guy took one of those, they sent him home in a baggie, if they found him at all. I was lucky, I just lost an arm. It was a good day for us because nobody got killed. Like we used to say there, 'It don't mean nothin'".

George's wife and family helped him heal, and helped him make it through the decision to amputate his right arm when the pain became unbearable.

"I still live with constant pain, but I don't let it get in my way. I've got the hook, and I can do pretty much anything that I could do with an arm. You never forget, and the wounds are way more than just physical. You may never stop looking for land mines, or being hyper-vigilant, or having occasional flashbacks and night-mares. But you can't let it get you, you can't let it run your life. You either deal with it, or it takes you down. I figure every day I'm here after I got hit, is a gift, 'cause the odds of me making it out of that one were pretty slim."

28 years later, his job takes him onto the streets of San Francisco, searching for the veterans society has chosen to forget. He is an outreach worker for the Homeless Veterans Center.

"I just go out and look under freeways, in abandoned buildings, in parks, anywhere they might be hanging out. I just want to find the vets that are out there living and dy-ing on the streets. If I can talk to them, and get them to trust me, I'll try and bring them to the center for help. Trust is the big thing, and it takes some time to get to that; these guys feel betrayed by the government and the system, so it's hard for them to believe anybody wants to help them. Once they see that somebody really does care, we can help them take that first step."

"I lost my arm in combat, but I see guys who lost an arm to drugs after they got back. Those are the guys that I want to help".

In speaking about the homeless community in the San Francisco Bay area, someone said of George Gibbs "he is the greatest gift", both as a person, and as an advocate for the homeless. Seeing the program and the people he works with, it is easy to see many would agree.

STEVE HAYDEN

1968-69 – 23 years old – Helicopter Mechanic/Door Gunner

*S*teve seems eager to be interviewed. He jokes with his boss as he takes a break from the homeless veterans training program where he now spends most of his time. The moment he begins talking about Vietnam, his voice and demeanor change. He sits with head down, eyes averted, hands shaking as he sips nervously on cup after cup of coffee and water.

"It was much worse coming home than it was being there. It was painful to see how quickly people turned on you. I was afraid to say I had been there, and had to submerge my identity. Pretty soon, I had no friends left, and I felt like I didn't exist, I was invisible."

"I had some of the happiest days of my life in Vietnam. I had a girlfriend over there, and I had a responsible job that I was damn good at. I didn't have a problem there. I was pretty f---in' normal."

Steve's anger becomes evident as his voice rises, and he is visibly more agitated.

"I feel like a foreigner in this country, except when I'm here with other vets. Everyone treats the Vietnam veteran like they don't exist. They don't want anything to do with them. None of you really understand, or even want to understand. How could you possibly understand what it feels like? You pretend that you're interested, that you actually care, that you want to hear what I have to say, but you don't. You don't care, nobody really cares what happens to anybody who was in Vietnam. Why do you want me to look at you? You don't want to see me. You'd rather look the other way."

Steve was homeless, but at the time of this interview, was living temporarily at a hotel. He is currently rated by the VA at 100 percent disability for Post-traumatic Stress Disorder. He is in a job training program and hopes to return to work.

ROGER WILLIAMS

1970-71 — 19 years old — 27th Transportation Battalion

R oger's parents encouraged him to "do his duty" so he enlisted.

"I drove a gun truck in a security platoon. We were responsible for the safety of others, and took pride in it. There'd be weeks of quiet, then all of a sudden it went crazy and our trucks were getting blown up everywhere. If I'd been my current age, 49, the hypertension would've done me in, but, being young, we got to be adrenaline junkies, even though we knew we could be killed."

They were always alert for ambush sites, and he brought that home

"It wasn't till about three years ago I was able to stop looking for ambush sites when I was driving on vacation up in the mountains, or on country roads. I'd catch myself looking for ambush sites, instead of at the scenery."

"Until recently, I thought about Vietnam every day. It wasn't all bad, but it was every single day. I've been trying to write down my thoughts about Vietnam in a journal lately. Not feelings, just thoughts, more in a detached way. I think it's been kind of therapeutic though."

Roger found he was short-tempered and irritable when he came home.

"After I came back I'd cuss at my mom, and argue with her, and my sister said I seemed nervous and wouldn't talk about it. I thought I handled it OK, but I know I was a jerk, impatient and short tempered. I treated my long-time girlfriend poorly too, which I really regret. We broke up, and I know it was me. We'd have screaming fights, and I'd throw things at her. I never struck her, but it was bad. When I was in Vietnam I made plans to buy a van and take a trip around the States with her. I got the van, was ready to go, and she got pregnant, so I convinced her to get an abortion. It bothers me to this day, that I was so self-centered and adamant that nothing would stop me. I took her to the clinic, and then just acted like we were back to normal when we got home. It didn't seem like a big deal at the time. Nothing did."

He also craved the stimulation he had when he was in Vietnam.

"I found some of that in drugs, but it wasn't enough. When I was over there, I worked with some MASH units, and sometimes helped them out when they got mass casualties. When I got back, I knew I wanted to work in the medical profession, and after I got fired from my old job, I got hooked up with an ambulance company. I got out of that, but now work on emergencies in hospitals. It's still life or death situations and I like that. Being an adrenaline junkie has taken its toll though; I now have hypertension."

"I used to be bitter towards the Vietnamese, then it turned into guilt and remorse. I felt sorry that we treated the people, especially civilians, like we did. We lumped them all into one category and wanted revenge for things they did to us, and I feel sorry we did and felt what we did. "

"I haven't been to the Wall in DC, but I've been to the traveling wall. It was very emotional. I looked up people I knew there, and just started bawling. It also made me think of another guy who died there, Immanuel Gomez. He committed suicide. He asked for help, and the company commander refused it, so he ended up killing himself. He just couldn't handle it anymore. That was the ultimate tragedy to me, because it probably could've been prevented. His name should be on the Wall too."

Roger is married, father of two, and operates a heart-lung machine for vascular surgeries.

JOHN McNALLEY

1967-69 — 22 years old — Navy Officer

"We were all raised one way, with certain basic beliefs. Then you go to the Nam, and those beliefs are destroyed, and it changes you. Forever. I thought I had dealt with it, but I went to the Wall, and it ripped me open like a can opener."

John feels guilt on several levels; not only for having been a part of the destruction, but also for not acting on his conviction that the war was wrong.

"I was raised in a conservative, Irish Catholic family, went to Catholic schools all the way through college, and was very patriotic. I believed all the propaganda they fed us about going in there to fight communism, to help them fight off the invaders. Then I got there, and found out *we* were the invaders. I was on a ship supplying bombs and bullets to planes and infantry. I didn't pull the trigger, but I provided the means to kill. I knew the government had lied, and it was wrong to be there, but I took the cowards way out, and turned my mind off. I didn't question what I knew was wrong-doing. I didn't have the balls to protest and go to jail."

"Guilt and depression are my two biggest dragons. I think I had those tendencies before I went, but the Nam pushed them over the brink. I just have the basic feeling that I'm a worthless, bad person, and feel incredible guilt. When I came home, it took me at least a full year for my mind and my feelings to turn back on again. I had shut down so far, I just wasn't there, I couldn't get it back. I had a hard time looking at myself in the mirror, a hard time living with what I had been a participant in. I guess I feel that even today. You can put it away, but it doesn't *go* away. It keeps coming back to haunt you."

John is very angry at the government, the politicians, who "sat in their cozy offices and used us, sent us out there to die."

"I protested the war when I got back, but it was too late. Who knows, maybe all the protesting did was make it worse for the veterans. Will we ever heal from this?"

John feels his visit to the traveling Wall (where I met him) and this interview have helped him on his road to healing.

MO NERLI

1969-71 — 27 years old — USO Associate Field Director

*M*o's real name is Maureen, but the Vietnamese people she worked with couldn't pronounce it, so they called her Mo. She developed a deep sense of caring for them, as well as for all the young servicemen she came into contact with in her 18-month tour.

"There were 20,000 non-military women in Vietnam, and we've never really been acknowledged for the part we played. I'm very proud to have been one of those women, to have helped in Vietnam. In the USO, our job was to be happy and smiling all the time, whether we were out in the field or in the club. We saw the pain and the death and everything, but we had to put it aside and make happy. We just tried to make them feel someone cared about them, keep their morale up."

Sometimes it was difficult to sustain their own spirits though.

"When you keep all those tears bottled up inside, it's a hell of a thing when it finally comes out. It's taken me 29 years, but in 1995 the dam broke, and everything just burst out, I was drowning. I thought my life was over, and I really thought about calling it quits. Because I was non-military, I couldn't go to the counselor that friends had recommended at the VA, and I was angry about that. So I kept telling myself I was fine, still making happy. But I finally had to admit I needed help, and I had a very good counselor, who helped me so much. It's been a great time of growth. I still have periods I go into a funk, and I just have to accept that it will always be there for me."

"It was the most important time in my life. The sense of helping, the comradeship. People I worked with there are still my family. Your senses and your emotions were all so alive, you were more alive than you had ever been. It all molded me into someone I didn't know I could ever be. It just changed me. Prior to going over there, my job was to go to press parties and work with all these artists and things like that. After Vietnam I realized how shallow all that was. I was reaching out to those young boys who were so far from home, and in such a horrible situation, and that just seemed like what I should be doing.   I will never be the same, nor would I really want to be the same. It has molded me into an activist, given me a different sense of priorities. It made me see that it's not what you have that's important, it's what you have to give, in reaching out to others.

She returned to Vietnam a few years ago to try to make peace with the memories she's carried for three decades.

"I went back to Vietnam a few years ago, and the first night, I could hear gunfire, and rockets, and tanks clunking down the road, and I could hear screams. It was all in my mind of course, but it was very real to me. The whole time I was there, I was just numb. Then the last hour I was there, I sat on this hill and looked over to where my friends used to work, and I could not stop crying. You just can't go through something like that and not be as profoundly touched as we all were."

ROB COMSTOCK

1968 — 20 years old — Navy Seabees

R ob joined the Navy at 17. He volunteered for the Seabees, looking for adventure, but knowing he'd probably go to Vietnam.

"One thing that bothered me was seeing all the damage done to the children, so I volunteered to put air conditioners in all the orphanages. We were behind enemy lines some of the time, and in some combat, but I tried to focus on more positive things, like doing stuff for the kids."

"I smoked grass every day when I was there. It was so available, so cheap; Vietnamese walked down the street carrying baskets of it, and you could just grab a handful. It made it easier to be in that situation, but I think I got addicted to it, so when I got home it was hard to stop. It was even harder quitting cigarettes. I started smoking those there too because we got them free in our c-rations. I got hooked, and they were even more addictive than grass."

"The thing I remember when I first got back was the bus ride. I had jungle rot, so I was on a hospital bus. It was dead quiet, and then a couple guys started crying. They were so amazed by the colors. It wasn't all green and brown anymore. It's amazing how being in a place like that, even for a short time, you really appreciate the little things of life that we take for granted. I guess you never look at life the same after that."

But he had nightmares and other challenges when he came back too.

"I had 33 jobs before I started working for myself. I'd work for a couple days, get pissed off and walk out. I only wanted to have fun I guess. The biggest change was in my personality. I was always easygoing, I got along with everyone. But when I came back, somebody would say something and I'd just take their head off. I got into a lot of fights. People would say stuff about Vietnam vets, call me a baby killer, tell me I was a disease, and a rotten person, without even asking what I did. They were wrong, and I took great pleasure in making sure they understood they were wrong. "

His Dad finally intervened when Rob put someone in the hospital.

"A guy spit on me, and I snapped. It cost me huge medical bills, and Dad was afraid I'd end up in jail. So he forced me to talk, and after crying and yelling a couple hours, we talked for two solid days, all day and night. He was in WWII, behind enemy lines, so he told me what happened to him, and it was so similar. He was crying, realizing the kind of stuff I'd been through, and seeing the similarities. He said he carried an M-1 carbine, and I had an M-16, but they both killed people, and war was still the same. It was a different place, different technology, but the same results. It helped that he understood. I saw I wasn't the only one that went through this. After I got back it felt like I was alone, defending myself. You wanted to go back there, where you had your buddies protecting you, watching your back. Here, I felt I was on my own, so I'd turn on them with whatever I had. It took somebody who'd been in a similar situation, 40 years before, to put it into perspective, how meaningless you really are in the big picture. He made me realize that instead of just being angry and wasting my life, I should appreciate that I came back and I better do something with my life. I don't know what would've happened if he hadn't done that. He saved me."

Rob makes fine period reproduction furniture. His workshop, and the gallery he operates with his wife, are in Door County, Wisconsin.

GREG BURHAM

1970-71 — 21 years old — Navy Seal

"Going over I had this idea I could help somebody. But my first firefight I realized I was only there to survive and help the people I was with survive. When I came back and tried to process that it was scary. I felt tainted, evil and condemned. I was prepared to put myself at risk when I went, but not for what it'd feel like to kill or hurt people, and where I'd put that afterward."

And he was shocked at the anger people had toward vets and the war.

"It felt very personal. People saw us as crazy, baby killers, waiting to go off. I was afraid of being found out, like I was some kind of animal. My big fear was, maybe I *was* that stereotypical vet people talked about."

"Going to school, it was hard to hear people who weren't there having esoteric discussions about the war or veterans. So I'd slide into the back row, trying to sneak back to normalcy without being noticed, going into sociology, where classes were big, and I could work on my own. A quarter away from graduating, I left, like I could get away from what was inside of me. I should have gone to therapy, but instead I walked from Alaska to Mexico, kind of a therapy itself. My body was a mess, but my spirit felt renewed, just letting go of all that anxiety about who am I and where do I fit in. People were kind."

In 1975, friends invited him to Denver, where he met his wife.

"She was the first woman not frightened away by my being a Vietnam vet. We moved back to Montana, and I worked with kids at a detention center, as a way to make up for the destructive time in my life; it was an atonement, a way to say, 'see, I'm a nice guy'. But I learned a lot about my vet experience working with those kids. My theory is we're all veterans of something, and their traumas put mine in perspective for me."

Then Greg and his wife had twins, followed by a year of sleep deprivation.

"All the unfinished Vietnam stuff perked up. My fear again, was I *was* that stereotype; given the right circumstance, could I revert to that person that hurt people, could I hurt my family? What I was really clear about was that I was *not* going to hurt anyone, so I fantasized how I'd take myself out if it ever got to that point. I was a mess, and wondered if I could ever be normal again."

"Finally a friend got me to go to therapy. I was way too confused to make that kind of a decision, and I still didn't want other people to know I had problems. But I felt like I was hanging onto my sanity by my finger-nails. Therapy helped me to start crying, and that was a real key. Up to that point it was the 'tears are not manly' thing. But therapy gave me permission to be angry, to grieve all the loss associated with Vietnam; not just the in-country stuff, but the whole script I had for my life before I went, that didn't work out. After I started doing counseling at the Vet Center, I had to go back into therapy for over a year again, because it brought up some old stuff for me. But helping other vets feels like good work, like I'm doing what I'm supposed to do. It's part of the gift of Vietnam."

"The sadness is part of who I am. I don't want to lose some of that. I don't want Vietnam to be a routine conversation, it's too important for that. When I went to the Wall that sea of names washed over me. My face was in the granite, and I looked for my name. Vietnam can bring me to my knees, but I think it's also a part of my strength. I don't think it will ever be over for me. It's an incredible burden and an incredible gift."

Greg counsels other veterans, does public speaking on the human costs of war and is happy in his role as father and husband. He was part of a delegation that went to the Soviet Union to help Afghanistan soldiers.

CHARLIE JAMES

1963-68 – Green Beret, Special Forces

Charlie brought his wife, Cupcake, to our interview, so I got the added perspective of a spouse, though Charlie did most of the talking.

"My daughter was 14 days old when I left for my first tour, and she was almost five when I came back. It was hard for my wife and kids, for all of us."

Charlie started his military career at 17, and was 28 by the time he did his first tour in Vietnam. He worked training South Vietnamese and Cambodian guerrilla forces behind enemy lines, and set up communications.

"I was in the service 22 years, until 1974. My last five years as a recruiter opened my eyes, seeing the public reaction to the war. I didn't want that job, but I was in Vietnam so many times, I think my wife and I would've split, or I would've been killed, if I went back. I got to be so hardened by what I was doing, and it cost me personally. But for what I did, I had to be that way. "

His wife adds, "When he went in, he was gentle and kind, with a lust for adventure. After Vietnam, he was so different; each time he came back he looked so much older, I almost didn't recognize him. He had a hardened look; the boy I knew was gone. His world shifted, there was a disconnection. It was hard to see him suffer, and hard not to give up on him. I was isolated; we didn't talk about it, and I couldn't talk to other wives, though they were probably going through the same thing. We were all too scared to say there's a good chance they'd die tomorrow, so we built up this fantasy thing where you didn't address any problems. Special forces divorce rate was over 85%, but I believed he was my soul mate, and if I got divorced, I'd still be stuck with him in my heart. So it was better to cope with it, and hope it got better."

Charlie replies, "What makes for a good soldier doesn't make a good husband. People that young shouldn't have to think about dying. Day in, day out, that becomes an unbearably heavy load. When I got home I was stretched to the breaking point, and got no help in readjusting. I got to a point where I really didn't care what I did, or what happened to me. I finally told my wife I was leaving. I don't know what I had in mind, just to get away. I figured I wasn't doing her any good anyway. I was drinking hard, and very saddened. I never smoked or drank before I went in the service, but after all I saw in Vietnam, drinking and leaving seemed to be the way to escape pain."

"Finally my wife found a counselor for me. I thought it was a joke, but I went along with it. He was older, and I respected him. He helped me put the cork in the jug and get my life together. I had planned to go to 26 years in the service, but because of the way I was, I decided to call it quits at 22."

"It taught me to be more forgiving and compassionate. I was forgiven for so much then, and I always try to help other vets. I still have a lot of sadness. I don't dwell on it, or live in the past, but I did things there I'm not proud of, and it saddens me the way humans can treat other humans. I can never say all the things I have inside, even to Cupcake. How could I burden someone else with such things? This is the first time I've been able to talk about it with someone who didn't want war stories, someone who only cared what it cost, and how it felt. It feels good to do that."

Charlie, his wife and daughter run The Sweetheart Connection, a singles magazine/dating service in Montana. In 1997, his daughter met and married a Vietnam vet named Randy Hall, through the magazine.

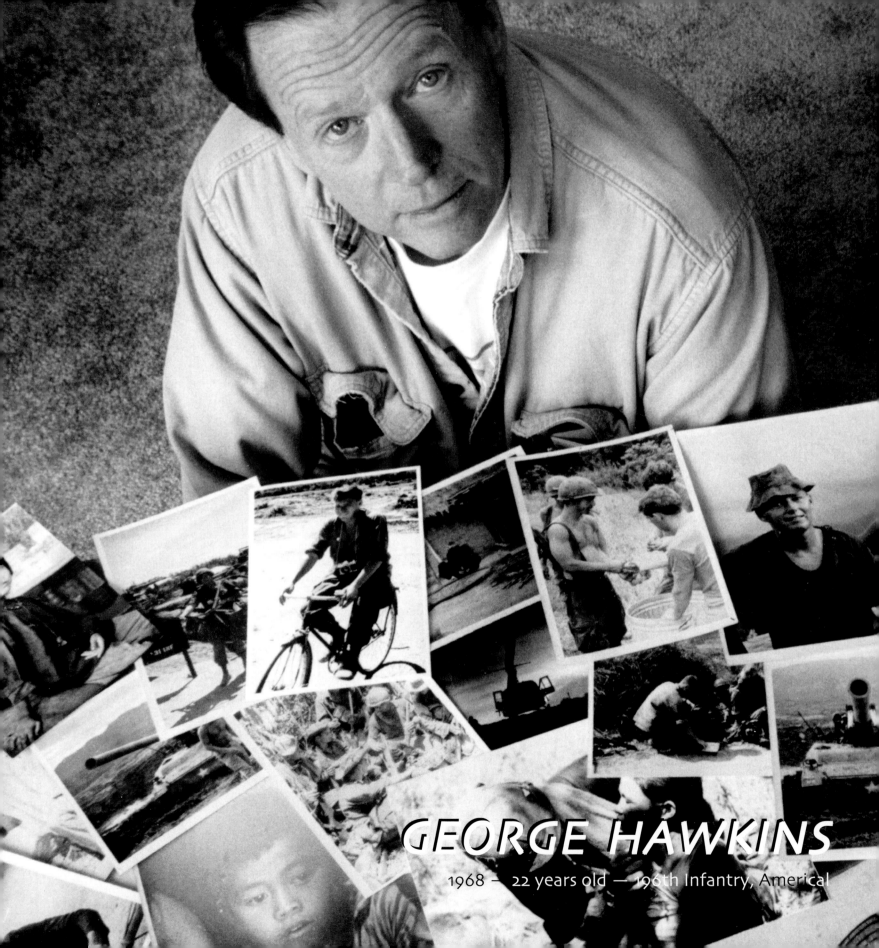

GEORGE HAWKINS

1968 — 22 years old — 196th Infantry, American

"When I first got in country I was scared to death, but after awhile you just accepted the insanity as your daily routine. I started out as a grunt, and then was able to talk my way into doing photography and journalism. "

Among the photographs George has from Vietnam, there are none of his friend Goodbody, except those in his mind. They had both graduated from college just before they got drafted, and found they shared a passion for literature. They became close friends, and whenever they had time, they'd talk about books, women, politics, and what they were going to do when they got back to the world.

"That was our escape, our way to blot out the reality we were caught up in. I gave him a book of short stories, and we both liked the passage at the beginning: "Cast a cold eye on life, on death. Horseman, pass by!" Goodbody believed the horseman symbolized death, coming to collect his bounty, with no emotion. He said he was going to do some writing when he got back to the world."

They were separated after many months but still met up occasionally in the field. They'd eagerly talk, share stories, and swap paperbacks and magazines.

"It was like seeing a brother for the first time in many years. Once, he showed me his new lighter, with the Yeats passage inscribed on it. I'd just bought the same lighter, and we laughed. I gave him a book of Frost's poems, just before his company went back to Que Son Valley, an NVA area he'd hoped never to return to. He tucked my book in the leg pocket of his fatigues."

Goodbody was walking point on Hill 205 on a dark night, and the NVA were at the top, waiting. Everyone broke and ran back down the hill. They had to leave his body there the whole next day. Two days later, George got on a chopper on Hill 445. Also onboard were two bodies going back to graves registration.

"Halfway back, the poncho covering one of the bodies blew back, partially exposing the face. It was Goodbody. I turned away, and looked at the blur of green and brown below. All I could think of was those three words, 'Horseman, pass by!'"

"We thought we were immortal. I'd hoped to develop a lifelong friendship with him, and his life, so many young lives, were wasted then. And it seems such a large number of people who did survive, wasted the life they were given after their experience there. I was grateful to be alive, but it was difficult coming back."

George had been accepted to law school before Vietnam, but when he returned, he found the idea of going back to school trivial and uninteresting.

"I didn't realize it at the time, but looking back I can see I was very depressed, and angry at the waste of life, for at least couple of years. I found it hard to concentrate or find anything interesting, so I kept changing jobs. They all seemed boring and insignificant. During that time, I wrote a book about the war, and Goodbody, and coming home. It was never published, but it was a very cathartic, therapeutic experience for me. It helped me get my feelings out. But my feelings were never quite the same since Vietnam. I find it's been very difficult to have close relationships since then. I guess you see how quickly it can be taken away. "

After our interview, George was finally able to find the real name of his friend Goodbody, something he's wanted to do for years. He plans to go visit his grave of Timothy Rizzardini, and possibly his family, over Memorial Day.

TIM BREEN

1969 – 22 years old – Army Security, Military Intelligence

"I got over there on April Fools day. I felt afraid the whole time, and betrayed; betrayed by my country, the system, the idea of patriotism, and by my school teachers who gave me this wrong notion of what America is and does. It destroyed my sense of trust. If you betray my trust, I just go ballistic.

Tim never realized how severely Vietnam affected him until he was evaluated at the VA for treatment.

"The physician asked me questions about Vietnam, and I opened my mouth, but no words came out. I physically couldn't speak. For years I stuttered, trying to get it out, until finally I could talk about it. I still have a lot of anger, and I'm not ready to drop that; it was my protection. I still lose sleep with it when it feels out of control, and I still sometimes think about killing people, and have to tell myself to back off. I can vent it in more acceptable, non-physical ways now. "

He drank before he went, and occasionally to excess, as most young people do.

"In Vietnam, I went pro. When I left there I was an alcoholic, and a marijuana addict, and I didn't draw a sober breath for 10 years. I got through school on short-term memory, so I have degree, but don't remember a thing. I was a philandering liar, not a nice person, and it ruined the relationship I was in. I was pissed all the time, and I looked for opportunities to fight, so I could get rid of all that rage. I graduated, and I went to inpatient treatment for alcoholism the next day. I was in three months, and I've been clean 18 years. I won't say I became an alcoholic *because* of Vietnam, but it was a large factor."

Tim hoped for some understanding or empathy when he came home.

"But America wasn't there for me. I was so enraged at the country, I was ashamed to be a citizen. I was glad to see Desert Storm was so well-executed, but when I saw the welcome home they got after a few days in combat, it just brought up all my rage, all my frustration. It's good the country did a welcome home vets day, but it was two decades late for me. Americans *still* don't want to talk about Vietnam, but when I travel, people are very interested in understanding my feelings and my experience."

"It took me many years to go to the Wall. I'm ashamed to say this, but there were Asians there, and I couldn't handle it, I wanted them to go away. I had to leave, and I came back about two o'clock in the morning. I've been back a couple of times, and I'm OK now. I've not looked for anyone's name. I can't do that."

"Vietnam opened my eyes to a different way of living and thinking, and began a lifelong interest in other cultures. Travel is one of my passions. If you try to understand a person who is different from you, you're far less likely to want to kill him."

"I've been given an opportunity to have some understanding of myself and the consequences of my life's path. I was the first guy in my family to go to school and to war, and I survived both. Since I did survive, I feel a responsibility to live my life well and do the right thing. I'm very fortunate. I've done well financially and have a marriage that is happy beyond my dreams."

Tim is currently travelling through Southeast Asia. He is in Thailand, where he took this self-portrait, and hopes to be able to revisit Vietnam. He fears the trip, but hopes to gain some understanding and healing, if he allows himself to go.

CATHLEEN CORDOVA

1968 – 20 years old — Army Special Services

C athleen was raised in a patriotic family, and volunteered to go to Vietnam.

"If our boys had to be there, I wanted be there to support them. I had no idea what I was getting into, and wasn't smart enough to be afraid."

She was assigned to run the service clubs, which she describes as a safe place for soldiers to get away from the war.

"It was just one year, but it changed my life, my direction, many of my fundamental beliefs. Guys would talk about horrible things that happened, and our job was just to listen, not to react or make any kind of judgment. That has to change you. It's like a bullet hitting a wall; it goes one direction until it hits, and then it goes all over the place. I had plans and knew exactly what I wanted when I left. Then I hit that wall, Vietnam, and didn't know where I'd land. Before I went, I wanted to go to grad school, and be a social worker in adoption. I was quiet and timid, into very traditional roles."

But she found school trivial after her Vietnam experience, and decided she didn't want to be a social worker anymore. Many employers wouldn't hire Vietnam vets, so it was hard to find a job, hard to readjust to the U.S.

"I was uncomfortable being here. It was like I left for a year and came back 20 years later. People on both sides of the war did horrible things to each other, then you came home, and no one cared. These kids were so young they couldn't even vote, so it would've been up to the citizens to do something, and they didn't want to hear it. Everything had changed, and I had changed."

So she went to Korea with Special Services, to readjust, and rethink her life.

"When I got out, I was in Alabama, and I saw an ad recruiting women for the police force. It was obvious they didn't want to hire me, but they had to, because they had quotas for women then. I was the first woman in a lot of positions I've had, in spite of harassment. Vietnam taught me to challenge the system, and challenge what I could be. It made me independent and self-confident in a way I couldn't have gotten at home. I became resourceful, so if you tell me something is impossible, I know otherwise. I knew if I survived war, I had the self-confidence and the motivation to do anything, and I had options. I haven't done any of the things I'd planned, and have no regrets."

"I didn't feel that 20 years ago though, and it's taken its toll. I'm not the trusting person I was, I lost faith in my religion, and in humanity, after what I saw there. That's made it hard to have a lasting relationship, and nearly all my close friends are Vietnam vets or people I worked with there. There's an incredible bond that forms when you share that experience. I can't explain the intensity, but it was life-changing. I guess it was being that close to life and death, talking to someone one day, and the next day they're gone. We had all these emotions, fear, sadness, even revulsion, but we couldn't express them. We weren't allowed to react normally, so we stuffed it all, and I think when you do that, it intensifies. Eventually it all comes bubbling out, many times in some inappropriate way. It totally changed my life, changed me."

Cathleen is on the police force in Pleasanton, California. She is president of Women's Overseas Service League, and helped form a speakers bureau to talk to schools about Vietnam. She was in a documentary on women in Vietnam, "No Time for Tears." One of her letters from Vietnam is inscribed on the Vietnam Veterans Memorial in New York, where she formerly lived, and included in a book called "Dear America: Letters Home From Vietnam."

KEITH POLLARI

1967 — 20 years old — Gun Battalion, DMZ

Keith returned from Vietnam and was discharged the next day, leaving him no time to adjust to the transition from DMZ to Minnesota.

"Some students saw us go by and gave us the finger, and I took it felt very personally. I felt ashamed. So I took off my uniform, put it in the trash, and said I'd just go back to the world and forget anything ever happened. And that's what I tried to do. I stuffed it, didn't talk about it. I treated it as a non-event. I made it a subject that wasn't open to my family or my wife or anyone else to talk about."

A few months later, he burned his draft card during an anti-war protest, expressing his feelings about the war, hoping to be accepted back into society.

"I was one of two vets there, so they brought me up to the podium. Then they introduced me as a 'repentant baby killer'. I felt so abused and manipulated. That was the thing that really closed the door. I withdrew completely. I had such a sense of shame, that a lot of us have, over what we willingly or unwillingly participated in or saw. It wasn't safe to make that disclosure, so after that I never acknowledged I was there, never talked about it, never watched the news. I used alcohol and drugs to escape, and didn't really know what I was escaping from. I had such a fear of being branded or not trusted because people thought I was psychologically unstable. Even now, if I did some criminal act, the first thing they'd say is that I was a Vietnam vet. I should have a big red V on my forehead.

He was finally able to come to terms with that part of his identity during a drive to raise funds for the Minnesota Vietnam memorial. It was the first time he'd associated with other vets.

"I was drawn there, and I met other vets who had a feeling of confusion, emotion they couldn't deal with, and the wives and friends of vets who were trying to understand and help. That's when I came home, I think. I saw the common thread between myself and other vets. You didn't have to be that tough guy and your buddy died in your arms to be entitled to feel bad. I found my feelings were not wrong or peculiar; other people had the same feelings of guilt and shame, but I never knew it. It was good to feel close to people and not feel alone. It was the first time I felt that, which I guess is why I was divorced."

"Drinking was a way to cope with my intimacy issues and lack of success in other areas. But I stopped in 1984, and I was stark raving sober for awhile. I don't know if Vietnam was the cause of my being an alcoholic, or what I'd be if I didn't go. But it gave me a cause, and I think I used it as an excuse for awhile."

Keith returned to Vietnam a couple of years ago to validate the experience, and to see what it was like under different conditions.

"It's like when you go to a historical place, you get a different feeling walking on that ground than you do reading or talking about it. So I had to walk on my own hallowed ground. I wanted to reach that level of emotion that I couldnt feel in any other way. I took my son, who was in high school, and it was very moving for him, seeing that piece of history, of my history, my life. It gave him a better sense of who I am, and of what we were faced with as far as duty and honor and what was right and wrong; I don't think kids have to deal with that now. Being able to walk the streets at night without fear, and being welcomed by the people, was very freeing, and helped me release a lot on other levels too. I also just wanted to make amends and put some issues to rest, to give something back. So I've been doing some work and some funding with a school in Dong Ha, and that feels good."

LARRY GOODMAN

1969 — 19 years old — Army

*T*he numbers are carved in Larry's mind as if it was yesterday.

"I arrived in Vietnam August 29, 1969, and I was wounded November 27. At 6:04 I was on the surgery table. I slept for three days, and spent my 20th birthday in the hospital. I woke up with my right hand gone ."

Coming home to a nation hostile to the war and its veterans, Larry's defense, like many vets, was to isolate himself.

"My style has always been to hide out. Being an amputee in a social situation where you shake hands, immediately created a difference, and made Vietnam the focus of the interaction. So it was a helluva lot easier to avoid the interactions. My kids would like me to be more social, but I just can't be. Like after my daughter's soccer game last week, she told my wife, 'He was there, but not really, he didn't talk to anyone. You know him, he just goes off by himself'."

This is just one piece of an attitude, a feeling, a way of being, born in Vietnam, and still manifest in his life nearly 30 years later. The hostile environment he returned to in the 70's fueled the anger and fear Larry felt in Vietnam.

"I won't give up my anger; it's what drives me, and I've used it to help other veterans get the benefits they're entitled to. Veteran entitlement is my passion, my way of releasing anger and breaking down a system that doesn't work. They send us to war, but won't take care of us when we get back."

Though his success rate is high, he can't make any money at it because of a law that limits lawyer fees for veterans to $10. His legal assistant position provides a good income, but he now has mixed feelings about working in the legal profession at all.

"It works well in law to be confrontive, but maybe it's not the way I want to spend my life. I think it's a poor model of how people should relate to each other. If I had both my hands, I'd be a stonemason. That's what I always thought I'd be."

Larry has since retired from the law practice because of his disability, but is still working on his own, in veteran entitlement law, assisting veterans in pursuing benefits claims.

ROBERT KILKELLY

1965-66 – 19 years old – Navy River Rat

I met Bob at the Women's Vietnam Memorial in Washington DC. He looked at the statue for a long time, and then said, "She's got the thousand yard stare. It's eerie ... she makes me feel like I'm there again."

"I arrived during the Christmas holidays, and nobody wants anything to do with a new guy. I was so scared and lonely, I don't think I'll ever forget it. It's part of what made Vietnam so peculiar, and so difficult, going over and coming home alone. We became so detached from everyone and from the events, that I know I still have that tendency to turn inward and to distrust others. And I always find myself pushing people away right before the holidays."

Bob spent his tour in Vietnam on the river, in an LCMB assault craft, and received several medals. He served with the Navy until 1970.

"When I got home, I drifted around, living in a van. I entered the VA in 1971, seeking help for stress, and acting out by crashing cars and trying to commit suicide. PTSD was unheard of then, and I gave up when the VA wouldn't help me. That's when I turned to drinking. I don't remember much about those years; I'd drink up to a case of beer and a fifth of whiskey a day, and often went a week without eating. It had the familiarity of surviving day to day in Vietnam. And the van was just like living in the steel box of the boat I served on. I lived that way for several years, and don't remember much of it."

Bob was finally able to receive help from the VA, and went through an alcohol rehab program there in 1978, and stopped drinking. He got married in 1981, and was able to complete an AA degree program in 1995. But the nightmares have not gone away. He was forced to quit in the senior year of a bachelor degree program, because of his PTSD.

"I feel the fear every day. The anxious feelings of remembering, the coldness of pushing others away if they get too close. Inside, I want to be like them, and be able to trust and feel. I miss the innocence and the ability to love like they still do. I have to work everyday just to live. Both the American people and the government made us feel abandoned. There was no safe place or person to be able to talk about the experiences; we were even shunned by our fellow veterans. The WWII vets called us crybabies, and the general public assailed us as baby-killers. People say get on with it, but I can't. Do people think I enjoy living in this hell?"

Though much of this interview was conducted at the Vietnam Memorial, Bob has been e-mailing me since that time. This is a recent email, "I've crashed two cars in the last year. I lose my sense of reality and black out. Anxiety is high. I'm confused. It's like getting lost and panicking. I'm really scared. I'm in therapy and on heavy meds which keep me in a stupor. I want to run and hide, I'm so afraid I'll hurt someone and not know about it."

Bob still tries to work 14 hours a week in a human services job, and is still married. He is on 50% disability for his PTSD, and has not yet been able to return to complete his bachelors degree because of interfering symptoms.

CINDY BROWN
AND

Heidi and Cindy were in nursing school during the Vietnam War. When a military recruiter came to the school and asked for volunteers, Heidi pushed Cindy's arm up . When I called Heidi to interview, it was a package deal: I had to interview them together.

H: I really believe the reason Vietnam hasn't affected me as much as it could have, is because we worked together. Working with the person who became my best friend - together for over 30 years now - that saved me.

C - When we started hearing about all the vets who have PTSD, I told Heidi I felt guilty I didn't experience that, and I wondered if I was suppressing something. But we figured out it was because we always talked about it, about our bad experiences. Many people came home and were totally isolated. They tried to talk to people, but unless you were there, it's very hard to understand.

H: It was so much harder when Cindy left after 10 months. It would've been a totally different experience for me there if we hadn't had each other, very lonely. Having each other, we somehow felt protected and safer.

C - It was good I left neurology when I did though; it was really getting to me. There were 18, 19, 20 year olds, paralyzed, on striker frames, where the person is sandwiched in between, so you can turn them. It broke my heart. The war became reality for me there. I couldn't have handled it much longer.

H - That was the difference between Cindy and I. She got to know their personalities, where I was in ER and there'd be more gore, and chaos and screaming, getting them to the OR. But I never got to know their name or bond with them, which was perfect for my personality, and really helped. So the impact of it was different for us in that way. That carried through to the work I do now, in anesthesia; I put them to sleep and don't spend any time with them, no chance to get attached; I found my niche in Vietnam.

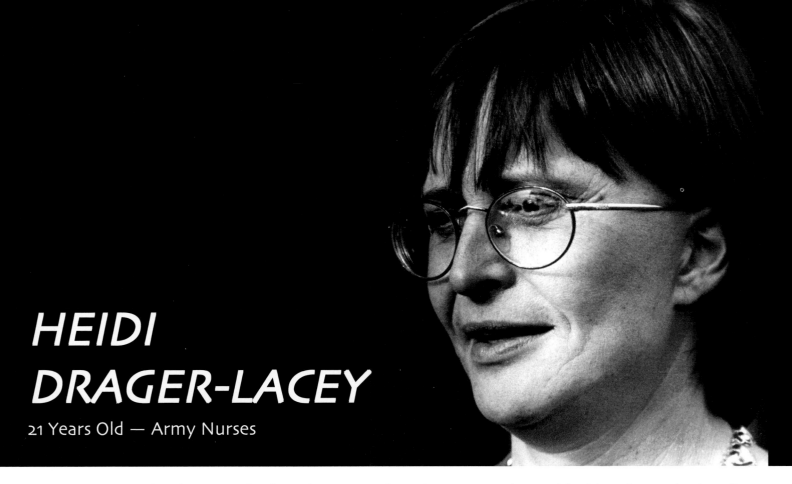

HEIDI DRAGER-LACEY

21 Years Old — Army Nurses

C - It was very hard to come back to the States after Vietnam. People would whine about a broken finger or something, and I'd want to quit.

H: When we came back and people found out we were in Vietnam, we got so much crap, from people who didn't know anything about it. At first, I'd argue about it, or make excuses. After awhile, I just wouldn't tell anyone.

C- People now are shocked when they hear I was in Vietnam, or even in the Army. They think of me as such a sweet, meek thing.

H - I wouldn't trade this experience though. We helped so many guys, and I felt special as a woman, too. They were just so thrilled to see round-eyes.

C - They never hassled us, though, and I never felt uncomfortable. In fact, I felt if anyone had tried to hurt me, they would've jumped out of bed with their broken legs and tried to protect me. I think they really respected us.

H: Going to the Wall was a totally overwhelming experience, and brought that all back. A guy I didn't know, just someone who'd been there, came up and hugged me, and there was a bonding there that was amazing.

C: We were close before we went, and our time there strengthened it so much. We can help each other work through anything, and we can validate each others experience there. It gave us a bond that can't be broken. We're inseparable.

Heidi and Cindy still work in nursing. They're both married, and Cindy's daughter is named after Heidi.

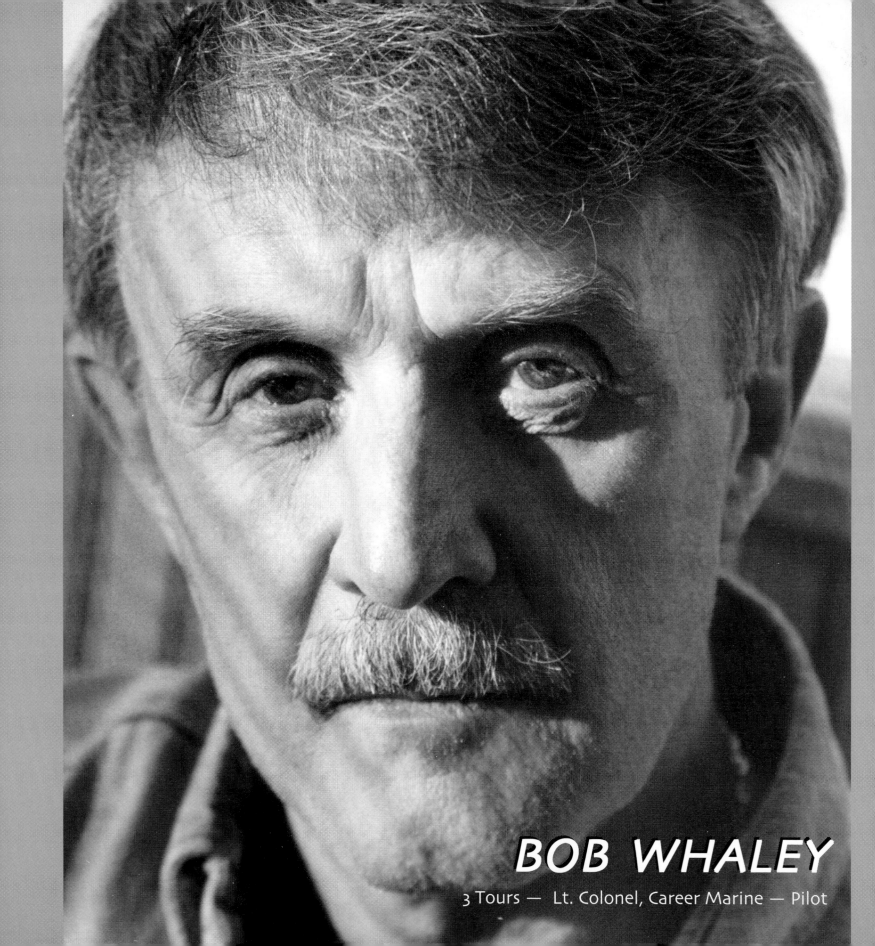

BOB WHALEY

3 Tours — Lt. Colonel, Career Marine — Pilot

*F*rom the time he was 10, Bob knew he wanted to be a Marine pilot.
"Watching the WWII movies, I'd play pilot all the time. I never smoked, and I always ran in school, because I knew if I ever had to escape and evade, I wanted to be in the best physical shape possible. I worked my way through college being a smoke-jumper, and that was exciting too. I didn't want there to be a war, but I knew if there ever was one, the Marines would be involved, and I'd be in the action, I'd be one of the first to volunteer."

He did his first tour in the Mekong Delta in 1962. His second, in 1965 in central Vietnam, was cut short by a serious helicopter (Huey) crash.

"That was the best part of Vietnam for me; I met my wife, a stewardess, on the plane on our way back to the States to recover. Then I did one more tour, flying the OB10's up near the DMZ. So I got to see it almost from the beginning, to when we were starting to remove troops in 1969. At the time, I thought our being there was the right thing, but I later realized the politicians were making decisions that were affecting the well-being of the military action. I saw some atrocities too, so I knew we weren't perfect. I was still in the military after Vietnam, serving one more overseas tour, so I was insulated from much of the experiences other vets had coming home."

"Vietnam was a very positive experience for me, very professionally challenging. It's gut-wrenching when you lose your buddies, but there's something about the make-up of an aviator; you know there's always that risk, but you're willing to take it. Every time I lost a buddy, I wrote his name, the date, and what he was flying in my book. I counted over 50 guys that I'd known, flown with, been friends with, that were killed while I was serving."

"I think anybody that's been there has scars from it. But the definition of a scar is a wound that's healed over, and I think I've pretty much healed from it. I'll never sit with my back to the door when I go out, and I still sleep with my loaded .45 next to me, in the night stand. That's about the only hang-ups I have, and it's not bad. But I know a lot of guys can't heal from it, and I think part of it is that I was a lot older than most when I went over. I will not judge other people for how they deal with it, because nobody can ever know what they went through. We had it easy as pilots; we had a hot shower and a bunk at night, while most guys were in the jungle, in crap they never knew if they'd come out of. There are some who blame Vietnam for failures, when in fact they might have failed anyway, and that's wrong. For them to use Vietnam as an excuse, which destroyed so many lives, is obscene. It invalidates all those who have problems that are justified and very real."

"I guess Vietnam was not totally worthless, if we view it as a bad example of how not to conduct a war. And it made me appreciate life and all living things more than I ever did. Since Vietnam, I've never been able to hunt again. I'm not really against it, but I just can't bear to shoot anything. I know how precious a life is now, and I can't bring myself to take one. "

Bob is still married to his Vietnam-era sweetheart, and works as a financial planner.

MARK MARKOWITZ

1967-68 — 26 years old – Air Force Flight Engineer

Mark was pursuing a career in the Air Force when he went to Vietnam.

"John Wayne movies was all I knew about war, so I was very macho, with this attitude of heroism and glory. I was excited to go to Vietnam."

Glory soon turned to fear, then to anger. The fear began on his first trip as flight engineer on a plane full of body bags, wondering if he would be one of the lucky ones to make it home alive. When he did make it home, it was to a world he didn't know.

"My daughter was one month old when I left. When I got back, I was so on edge, I couldn't even be around her, and she didn't know who I was."

"I wasn't sure who I was anymore either. I went over feeling macho and aggressive, and came back wimpy, with no self-esteem. I couldn't stand up to anybody, couldn't defend myself or my opinions. I went over with a strong sense of spirituality, but when I came back I knew there could not be a God. Before I went, I was a good Jewish boy who obeyed all the rules. But when I came back, I was looking for the excitement and tension I had in the war. I found it by getting into trouble, one thing after another, everything from adultery to theft."

"I've been divorced four times...I was in constant turmoil, and couldn't keep a relationship. I got in so much trouble, I ruined my career in the Air Force and had to leave. Then I stole from my employer, and I stole from other people, too. I could easily be homeless or in jail now, if I didn't have a sister who cared about me, and wanted me to come and live with her."

After his last divorce, Mark moved to San Francisco, where his sister has a small apartment, and began to repair his life. He volunteers, has started therapy for his PTSD, and has found his spirituality again.

"I'm still overcome by rage at times, and I don't know why. I've broken my hand hitting a concrete wall, but I never hit a person. I get so depressed, I sit and cry for hours and can't leave the room. But I have three good friends now, and they'll come and drag me out for coffee or something. They respect me, and that's helping me respect myself again. When I first started counseling at the VA, I felt so alone, like I was the only vet to have these problems. It was like a ray of sunshine when I met your husband, and found out I'm not alone, and there is hope."

BILL ROMEO

1969 — 28 years old — Intelligence Officer

*B*ill received his draft notice after college. He decided to enlist, which enabled him to go to OCS. He was eager to serve, and had a positive attitude.

"Before I went over, I belonged to a fraternity, loved to dance and party, ran track, had lots of friends, and was a real happy-go-lucky guy. When I got there and saw what a sham it all was, how much we had been lied to, it just changed me. It made me very untrusting, emotionally distant, and cynical. I have friends who weren't put through that meat grinder, and they're still the happy person I used to be. It altered our brain chemistry, just as other traumas can. I also had a severe back injury from a chopper crash, so I came back both physically and mentally wounded."

Like many veterans, Bill didn't feel he belonged anymore, and wasn't really sure he even wanted to.

"When I got home, I grew my hair long, got a motorcycle, and just went crazy. I built an A-frame on 15 acres in the woods of Vermont, and lived without a phone or electricity. Everyone was wary of us, and maybe they should've been. When you're in a war, and 24 hours later you're back in society, expected to bow to authority and follow the herd, of course you'd be different. You've learned to survive and think for yourself, so you don't believe all the crap they hand you. I was confused with all the protests, and started wondering if I did the right thing. I felt rejected and guilty. I didn't know it then, but now I recognize the symptoms of PTSD."

Eventually, friends intervened, and he sought help at the VA. He then returned to school and earned Masters and Doctorate degrees in psychology.

"I'd never imagined doing that, so that's a positive thing that happened as a result of Vietnam. I worked in the field until my job was cut, then went back in the military. But my back and my PTSD got worse again, and I was medically retired in 1985. My psychology training has helped me to understand what's happened to me with the PTSD. It's a healing process much like if I'd had a limb amputated, but I think something physical like that is easier for people to understand, because you can see it. The wounds of PTSD, you can't see."

"I was married when I was there, but it was tough after I came back, so my losses include wives as well as friends, and I'm in pain every day with my back. But it got me off the group-think track, got me out of beer and sports, and made me realize I could think independently and creatively. I started painting and sculpting when I first got back, and painted 36 landscapes the first year. I guess it triggered some kind of response to block out the craziness of war and civilization. You have to do something with the anger, so instead of turning it inward and being depressed, or outward and being aggressive, I turned it into art. I take old rusty pieces of scrap metal, and turn them into something new, make them into art. I think people are like that; they can renew themselves."

Bill is divorced, living in Montana, writing poetry and doing his art in the basement of his home.

ALLEN MORGAN

1970-71 — 23 years old — Captain, Army helicopter pilot

*A*llen's unit flew mainly South Vietnamese soldiers, since the Army of South Vietnam had few pilots.

"We were in one battle in Laos where nearly all of them were wiped out… some of their finest soldiers. Only 22 out of almost 500 survived. Many of us felt it was *set up* to be a losing battle, part of a plan to shorten the war by wiping out the South Vietnamese in battles they had no chance of winning. I felt betrayed, especially when a colonel said we actually lost less helicopters there than he thought we would. They were sending us in there to die."

Two weeks after he got back from Vietnam he married a woman he'd met when he was going to officer's training school.

"I did a lot of drinking and drugs then, and I had to smoke pot just to sleep at night. For a long time, the only place I could sleep at all was on the couch, because I was having so many nightmares. My mom said I'd changed when I came home, but I couldn't see it. I guess she was right because the marriage only lasted a couple years. I felt totally alone. Some of my close high school friends said some really ugly things to me when I got back, so I lost that part of my youth, I lost my friends, I lost my wife. No one could understand because they hadn't been there."

"So I moved to California and got a job through friends as a sales rep. It was OK for a long time because I could move around and not have to deal with a boss or be confined to an office eight hours a day, so I could conceal my depression and anger. I had flashbacks and nightmares, did drugs, but somehow I managed to keep up the facade. During that time I also got married again, and had two great kids, but I again divorced several years ago. Since then, I've been through a series of ups and downs with depression, and had a hard time keeping a steady job. I was desperate, and finally went to the VA for treatment about three years ago. It was hard because I don't feel I can trust the government at all. "

One of his treasured memories is the close relationship he had with a Vietnamese photographer who was killed along with a U.S. photographer.

"He'd given me a lot of his photos, and I kept the one I thought was his best, to remind me of the insanity and the horror of that time. I saw a definite change in myself from seeing the beauty in things to seeing only ugliness. You try to keep some type of sanity, but you finally realize there is no sanity."

"I'm just now getting to the point that I'm even able to look at that chapter in my life. It was much too painful before, and I've seen other guys that were totally destroyed. A kid from my high school that was voted most likely to succeed went to Vietnam, and ended up killing himself when he came home. People don't realize it not only destroyed guys who were there, but also families, girlfriends, and wives. They had to fight our battles when we came home."

The official government stance during the Vietnam War was that U.S. Troops were never in Laos at all.

Allen lives with his son in California, and feels he has finally begun his healing journey. He is a computer consultant.

DAVID LYMAN

1966 — 26 years old - Photojournalist, Navy Seabees

David was one of the very fortunate people who had a totally positive experience in Vietnam, both personally and professionally.

"Vietnam was one of the key periods of my life, and I look back at it with fondness. It was a challenge that I met. Like many guys, I was hoping to be challenged as a man, to find out if I had the courage to do what it takes. But I also had the opportunity to photograph and write stories, which is what my profession was. I went all over Vietnam doing stories for the Seabees, and publishing a newsletter. I was lucky, I got out of Vietnam every month to put together this newsletter, so I had a lot better time of it there than most guys."

The unit David was in was made up of older guys, trained in civilian life as construction workers. They built schools, houses, and other buildings for the Vietnamese, so they were mostly in non-combat areas.

"We were in a very protected area, and it was like MASH. It wasn't my job to kill people, just photograph them. We got in a few scrapes, and almost got blown up a few times when we went over land mines, but I was very lucky. Although the personal challenge didn't match what I was secretly hoping for, it was definitely a great professional challenge. I don't think there's a journalist alive that wouldn't jump at the chance to go to a war, so I didn't go there begrudgingly. I was excited at the opportunity. Vietnam really did set me up for the rest of my professional career. "

"Before I went I had no political consciousness at all. When I saw what we had done, I came back angry at the US government for getting involved and keeping it alive for so long. That war was primarily a playground for a bunch of generals, their last chance to play at what they had always been trained to do. The Vietnamese didn't want us there, and we did a lot of harm, wasted a lot of lives, and a lot of money."

David used his experience in Vietnam to enable him take risks, and to be bold in his aspirations, and his professional decisions.

"My experience there made me realize I could do anything. When I wanted to take photography workshops and found that no one was offering what I wanted, I decided to start my own school. It's now the largest summer photography and film school in the world, and we're an accredited college. I never graduated from college, and now I own one. We've built a program for people who for whatever reason, can't make it in the regular academic world. I feel like my experience there gave me the confidence to know I can do anything I put my mind to, a different kind of courage than what I thought I was looking for. It also allowed me to help a lot of other people to realize their goals, to take courageous acts in their own lives. "

David owns the Maine Photographic Workshops, in Rockport, Maine. He recently remarried and had his first child, the beginning of another adventure.

PETE LAWRENSEN

1969 — Army Ranger, Advisor to Vietnamese Battalion

Pete went to Vietnam on his 20th birthday, and came home on his 21st.

"I had two really close friends since grade school, who died there. I went to the Wall, and the photographs at the bottom of the picture above my desk are their names on the Wall, so I can never forget. They were the closest friends I ever had.

" I knew I didn't have the money or the mindset to go to college then, and I thought if your country needed you, you went. I was supportive of the military, and felt those who went to Canada were wrong. But when I got out in '72, troops were coming home, and we all felt what we did was for nothing. When they released the POWs I cried, and it was the first time I admitted the government had lied to us. I was still supportive of the military, but mad at the government and the protesters. I thought they weren't dealing with it, but in reality, I was denying I was involved in it. I did that till the mid 80's."

Pete was angry, "screwed up", and had the capacity to be very violent.

"I'd punch a hole in the wall, or throw a lamp across the room, and just by the grace of God, I was able to keep from unleashing that anger physically on my wife or another person. My dad never got rid of his baggage from WWII, and took it out with drinking and physical violence. I swore I'd never do that, but I came so close. I finally went to the vet center and spent two solid years in counseling. I came full circle, and was glad when Nixon gave amnesty to the guys who went to Canada. I became active in veterans affairs, so instead of denying my involvement, I displayed it. But I had survivor guilt; why did my best friends get killed and I didn't? It made me realize the word communism is not a good enough reason to sacrifice all those lives."

Pete feels his experience in Vietnam made him more compassionate, and more open to people who look or live differently.

"I had a great deal of respect and compassion for the Vietnamese, which has carried over to all people. None of us gets to choose our lot in life, and many of us aren't given the opportunity to do better. But it's easy for people who are doing well to be critical of somebody who's different. Vietnam taught me not to judge people by how they look or what they sound like. We're all just people."

"I learned it's OK to be sad and to cry. I still feel a great deal of sorrow and don't ever want to lose that. I became aware of how fragile life is, how precious, and the tragedy of losing a life. I've become very close to the parents of one of the friends I lost in Vietnam, and though it's been 30 years, they still feel as much anguish as they did then. They'll die feeling that."

"I go to the high school several times a year and talk to kids about war. I try to keep it positive, but they need to know what it's really like. Especially young boys, mesmerized by the uniform and the glory. They need to know it's young boys just like them who get killed in a war, If we don't pass this on, then they just see war in the movies, and don't realize the personal toll."

"It's pretty close in my mind and heart almost every day, and I don't really want to ever lose that."

Pete is the Chief of Police in Missoula, Montana.

SHIRLEY AND

*S*hirley does most of the talking, and Frenchy, with his heavy Cajun accent, interjects his comments, and nods in agreement. Shirley has spent a great deal of time, personally and professionally, investigating the impact Vietnam has had on her life, her relationship, and other women who served there.

S — "Frenchy and I were the first married couple to be stationed in Vietnam together. Although I was an officer and he wasn't, I managed to get myself assigned there five months after he went over."

Shirley didn't even see herself as a veteran, but she did see Frenchy as one

"Recently, I published a research project I did on women vets, and found we didn't feel we had a right to say anything about Vietnam, because we weren't on the battlefields. But we did so much in Vietnam, and the relationship between nurses and doctors was one of trust and respect. I came back feeling like I could do a whole lot more than what I was given credit for, or allowed to do here. So I became a nurse practitioner, then got my Ph.D. The experiences I had there changed my whole direction."

F — "I was pretty bad by the time she got over there. I drank a lot more there so I didn't have to worry about getting shot, and if Shirley hadn't been there, it would've been even worse. It made me love her more, 'cause I was always worrying about her. I just kept drinking so I wouldn't worry, or even know I was in Vietnam. I became an alcoholic there."

S— "We can laugh about it now, but we had some bad physical fights there. One time he thought he'd knocked me out, but I was pretending so he'd stop hitting me. (she laughs) He thought he'd knocked me out, so I got anything I wanted for the next couple weeks."

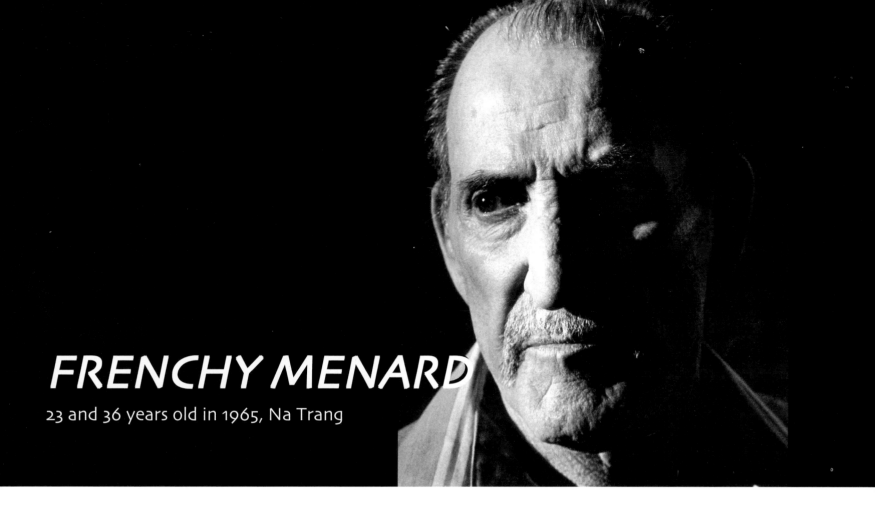

FRENCHY MENARD

23 and 36 years old in 1965, Na Trang

F— "I was banging her head on cement. That was bad."

S— "When we got back, his drinking and temper got even worse, but we stayed together till I was afraid for our daughter. I said choose the drinking or us, and he quit. I'm very proud of him for that. It took a long time for us to regain what we'd lost during that time. We could've easily broken up, but we had this strong commitment. It was Vietnam that kept us together because it created this amazing bond. It made me almost fanatical about our marriage."

S — "Overall, Vietnam was a negative experience for Frenchy, positive for me professionally, and a real mixture for the relationship. It was such an extreme experience and so terrible, but in the middle of all that was love. I think that knowing that he could be lost, he could die, at any moment was the thing that created such a strong bond between us."

F — "There was always a fear that you could die any minute."

S — "We've been married 34 years. We shared something in Vietnam that's very deep, and I really doubt we'd be together if we hadn't had that. I go to the wall every time I'm in DC, and I know there are people I lost over there, but I can't remember one single name, though I remember cases. I've just buried a lot of Vietnam. I guess that was my protection."

Frenchy is retired from the military. Shirley still works in the medical field, and is on the Governor's Commission for Women in Texas.

JOHN STANFORD

1969 – 22 years old – 4th Infantry Medic

"One of the things I value most since Vietnam is a toilet. I had to dig the hole every day, that we'd use for a toilet. And every time I had to use it, I'd be scared I'd get shot while I was sitting there. Now, I'm not sitting on a sandbag, and nobody's shooting at me. I really value being able to use a toilet without fear of dying."

John was a medic, only in Vietnam three months when he was wounded.

"Being wounded was a blessing in some ways. I did okay, dealing with being there for three months, but if I'd had to do it for a whole year, I honestly don't think I would have been able to handle it. "

For a medic, handling it meant crawling on the ground, over other bodies, to get to the wounded, always going toward the front, where the wounded would naturally be. John feels like he did a "pretty good job" in all the other firefights they were in, but feels intense guilt over the last one.

"So many people were killed that day, and I feel like I didn't do my job well enough. Our point unit got hit, and many were killed immediately. Our platoon got cut off from our company, and we were being bombarded from every direction, with rockets going off, and VC everywhere, even in the trees, shooting at us. I got wounded about nine in the morning, and we had no ammo left. I still tried to get to people for awhile, even after I was wounded; but then we were pinned down, and I couldn't move for hours, so I couldn't get to anyone. We were in there till midnight, and we couldn't move. But that was my job, to get to the wounded. I just went into survival mode, and I couldn't move. I might've been able to save a life, and I blame myself for those who died. I'll have to deal with that guilt the rest of my life."

Before he got to Vietnam, his vision of it was like the old movies.

"That's all a kid knows about war. But the first time we got in a firefight and my commander yelled 'Wounded! Get your ass up front medic!' and I was running up there, with my heart pounding out of my chest, it became a terrifying reality. This was not how it was in the movies."

"The firefight the day I was wounded was the most scared I've ever been, and I was absolutely sure I was going to die there. I'm a skydiver, and I was then, and I've had 13 parachute malfunctions in over 3,500 dives. I've been in a serious plane crash, where others were killed. But that day, that firefight, that was the only time I ever thought I was dead."

"No one can begin to imagine how it was if they weren't there. But what if you got 100 friends and gave them guns, and I got 100 friends with guns, and we all went out in the woods and hid, and tried to kill each other. Just try to imagine how you would feel in your gut and your heart. It's beyond terrifying."

"I've never been affected to the point of not being able to work or having constant nightmares. It's more a quiet grief that I'll have to deal with all my life. It's little things that trigger me, and I lose it. When I saw Platoon, the movie itself wasn't bad, but at the end when it said this movie is dedicated to all the guys who lost their lives over there, I lost it. It just brings it all back. "

John is married, and lives in Texas. He is a professional photographer, and designs and markets photo gear.

FRED DUBOIS

1969 — 20 years old — Army, Helicopter Gunner

"On a helicopter, we lived by the seat of our pants every day, scared out of our wits, and it made me not care about anything but survival and getting home."

When he did get home, he was very intense and angry, fighting constantly.

"So I went to the north end of Hawaii, and I just lived on the beach, by myself, for six months. I had a mask and snorkel, a speargun for fish, and an old broken refrigerator I buried in the sand. It helped me a lot. I thought I had it all together, so I came back here, and got in a fight my first day back in town. My family and everyone told me I was different when I came home, but I thought I was the same."

An incident with his Dad highlighted just how much he had changed.

"Dad and I were really tight, but even he said I was nuts. I remember goin' to his house two weeks after I got back, wanting to watch the news; I had buddies there and wanted to see what was goin' on. He said he was tired of all this Vietnam stuff. That was the first and last time I ever put my hands on my father. He changed the channel, I got pissed and put it back on the news, and he told me to forget about it, get on with my life. I threw him on the floor and got in his face, and I'm still apologizing 30 years later. To him, he got his son back, and it was over. But I got shot at every day for a year, and saw a lot of stuff, so it wasn't that easy. It's like if you got in a car accident, even a fender bender, every day for a year. Think about it."

He sought help once, for a recurring dream about a troubling incident where they had to destroy a village that had decimated another American company.

"As a helicopter gunner, you don't see anybody, you just shoot. So, we're shooting and this old papa san comes out right in the middle of this burning mess, and he's yellin and screamin, waving a rifle. My pilot kept yellin' at me, "Take him out, take him out!" and I said, look at the poor guy, we just destroyed his village and probably his family. The pilot just kept yelling at me to take him out."

He went to a vet center group for help, hoping to stop the haunting dreams.

"They were all whining and saying the government owes me. So I left and told them to get a life, and I just rode it out. But still, every single time I hear a helicopter, I think of that guy, I see his face. So I have to direct my mind, and get real busy real quick, so I don't go there. That'll never go away."

Fred's anger endured several years, and the apathy persisted even longer.

"I still didn't give a s--- about anything. I didn't care about getting ahead, or having a relationship, or voting, or any kind of rules. Like I didn't think I needed a drivers license; if I was able to drive, I was just gonna do it. Rules just pissed me off. In Vietnam there were no rules, you just did it. Christ, you get a 19-year-old kid, give him all the fire-power he can handle, and give him a green light, you're gonna have problems later. It just made me angry and aggressive when I got back."

"I was like that for 10 years, and the only reason I even started thinking about getting normal and thinking about tomorrow, was I met Nancy. I just didn't care about anything for 10 years; then I met her and all of a sudden I started caring what I said and did for her. I saw that she was a giver, not a taker, and she'd call me on stuff. She saved me, she gave me purpose, and a reason for doing things different."

"I know some guys who didn't make it back, and some who made it, but they're really screwed up. I think the guys that didn't come back are better off; they check out young and don't have to go through all that crap the rest of their lives. I've got a lot of good friends who are vets, and there's some that just can't let it go. I've been blessed my whole life, thinking if you got a problem, you find a way to get rid of it, and I was finally able to do that with Vietnam, but it took me 10 years."

Fred has been married to Nancy 20 years, and owns a contracting business.

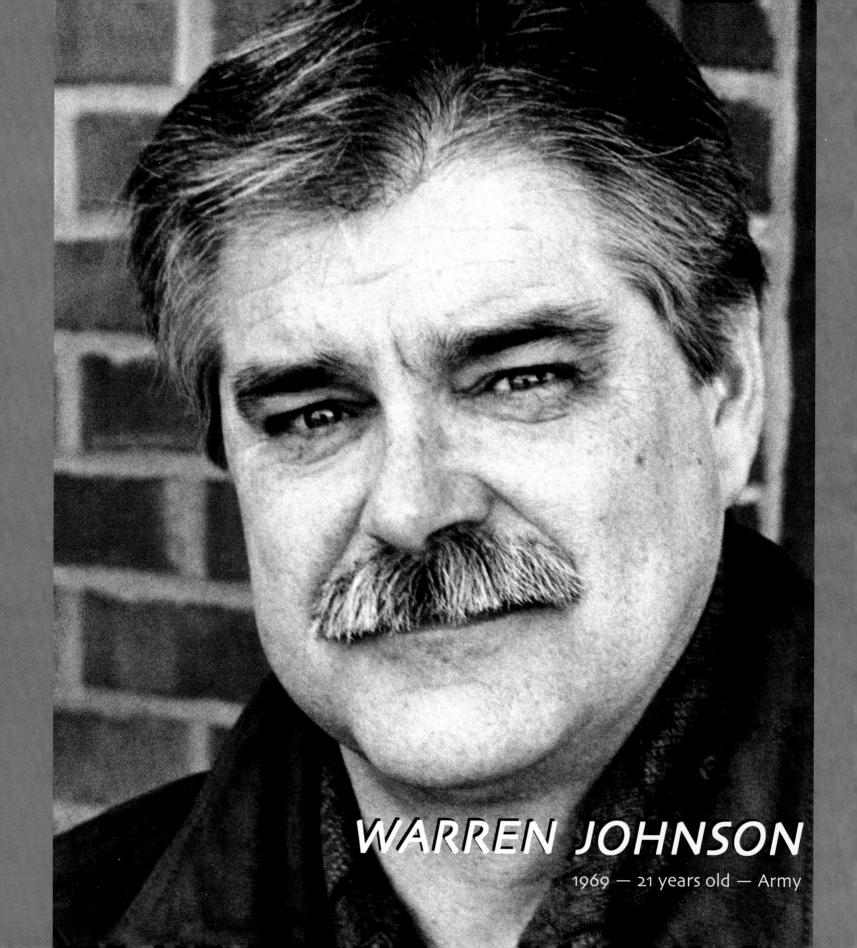

WARREN JOHNSON

1969 — 21 years old — Army

Warren married Connie just before he left for Vietnam. She says he was so sure he'd die there, he couldn't even tell her he loved her when he left.

"I had visions of saving the world from communism," he says, "but I ended up getting stuck being a guard at Long Binh Jail for 15 months. While I was there we had our first child, and I missed the first 10 months of his life. "

Like many veterans, Warren was not aware when he returned that he was any different than when he left, but to his wife, it was painfully obvious.

"I married somebody different than who came home to me," she says "When he left he was kind, loving, and sincere. He came back opinionated, sarcastic, cruel and self-centered, and he spent very little time with us. His life was partying and drinking; he would lie, and not come home. He was bitter and angry, very much a loner. He lost the interest and ability to make friends. His drinking got so bad, so pathetic, I didn't even like him as a person, didn't love him for awhile. He was a sorry excuse for a man. After 5 years of this, I had enough. He refused to go to counseling, but I went, and got strong enough to know I could take care of our 2 boys alone. I knew I'd regret it if I didn't try, so I set a time limit, and said if things didn't change, I was going to leave. About the same time, he got a DWI, and that was a wake-up call for him too. So things started to change then, but it took at least another five years until we were really OK again. We had made wonderful plans for our life, but after Vietnam, life was never really normal for him, and many of those plans didn't materialize."

He was working at Coke when he got drafted, but planned to return to college or have a career with the Highway Patrol when he came back.

"But I didn't want to go to college anymore," he says. "and you had to be gone a few months for the Patrol. Since I'd just been away from my wife and son for 15 months, I couldn't do that. So I just went back to work for Coke because it was easy. I regret missing that opportunity. I would've been retired now, with a pension more than what I'll ever make working here."

What hurts Warren most about Vietnam is losing a life-long friend.

"My friend Bob Lindgren, my friend since kindergarten, was killed two days before my 21st birthday, at Hamburger Hill. Years later I saw a preview on TV of a movie about Hamburger Hill. My son Sean asked if I'd heard of it, and I ran into the bathroom, weeping uncontrollably. He was so scared and kept apologizing, thinking he'd said something to upset me. It took awhile to compose myself, and reassure him he hadn't done anything wrong. When he was 18, he was going to D.C. on a soccer trip, so I asked him if he could do a rubbing for me at the Wall, on Bob's name. When he got there, he was too emotional, so he had to have a friend do it for him. He just broke down. He wrote me a letter while he was there about how hard it was, what it meant to him, and how proud he was I went to the war. That meant a lot to me, so I framed it and put it on our wall."

"We have three grown sons now," Connie says," and he's a wonderful Dad. We honor him for his service, and we are very proud of him."

"The rejection by the people of this country was very painful when I came home," says Warren. "But all that matters to me now is that my family, especially my sons, are proud of me and my service to my country."

Warren's son's letter is on the next page.

Dad,   Tues. July 2, 1991

I suppose you didn't expect to hear from
me in a letter. Well I had to write you.
I'm not going to talk about the Vietnam
Memorial, because I have to tell it to
you. I ~~got~~ got, ~~well~~ well Jeff did I couldn't,
a rubbing of your friend. I had a photo copy
made and am sending you that. I didn't want
to trust the mail with the original. Dad you
would be really proud, it was beautiful. That's
all I'm going to say. I picked up a couple
of postcards for you. They are not ~~staged~~
~~also~~ by a professional under perfect
conditions, it is really like that. You were
right, Dad, I couldn't handle it. I totally
broke down before I even came to the wall.
I want to go there tomorrow because I
feel a sense of warmth & belonging there. It
feels as if a part of me is there, because
so many parts of you are there. Thank you
for fighting for me. There are really a lot who
appreciate it. If you go there I would like to
go with you. Believe me, you will need help.
I would not have made it without my friends.
It was incredibly beautiful. I love you Dad.

                                          Sean.

JEFFREY BU

1967-68 – 18 years old – Mar

s sitting on a bench next to the driveway, waiting for me. He told me later he oft
guard, standing watch.

etnam, I don't really sleep. I guess someone has to be on watch. I never slept o
ou get killed that way. I'll never understand how a few months in any place can p
ther people. When they told me I was going home, I started bawling. I don't
o stay, but I didn't want to leave. It was all I knew."

amp Pendelton three months when I got back, and I didn't hang out with the guy
weapon clean, same as I did in Vietnam. So they put me in a locked ward for c
happens *after* combat. While you're there, it's normal, it's your life, violence is nor

I wasn't as disturbed by the combat experience as I was by the world, the hostile people. So I didn't talk about it, they didn't want to know. They didn't want to see me, I didn't want to see them."

"So I bummed around, went to school, quit, kept moving. There was no place to go but I kept moving. After the horror of Vietnam, there was this emotional boredom, and you didn't want to get close to anyone. Then I found alcohol and drugs; that was good because then I slept, and it kept the dreams away. I started hanging out in dark bars, drawn to the seamy aspect of the streets. It was comforting somehow, very base. It connected to what was still churning strong within me, which was combat, Vietnam. Street life had that edge, that danger. You'd get paranoid, but not really; it's a heightened sense of reality, like an adrenaline rush. Insecure environments were secure."

He quit doing drugs, but only quit drinking five years ago.

"The booze wasn't working, it was killing me. I'd get drunk and shoot holes in the ceiling. I was losing it, and I knew if they came for me I'd shoot myself, or them. I sat in the house one night with my .45 to my head, tired of trying to make things make sense. But then I thought, I lived through so much, it seemed like a coward's suicide. Fear is powerful; you control it or it controls you. I don't try to forget, I try to remember and can't. I am on 100% disability for PTSD. I can't get rid of it but I can control it. I'm on and off of meds, like anti-anxiety drugs. The anxiety attacks are the worst; total loss of control, like standing naked in a mine field. There's just certain things, some stimuli I have to avoid. That's why I like to do art; its creating something and it helps me leech some of the confusion. It was also a good cover for being an alcoholic and a vet. If you're an artist you're allowed to be a little odd."

"I've never talked this much about this s---. I've learned nobody gives a s---. And why should they? It's something that only the people who were there can share. Some cope and some don't, and it's not a sign of weakness, its a sign of sensitivity. Was I cold-hearted or was I too emotional?"

"My experiences in Vietnam are in a way the greatest thing I have. I feel time and indifference are destroying them, destroying me. The experiences are mine, my medals, my flag. To be a veteran is a possession, it's ours to hold. They may be losers, drunks, whatever, but they have *honor*. When I went to the Wall, I kept wondering if my name is on there. Those guys didn't come back, but I'm not really back either. I'm not really here."

Jeffrey lives with his third wife, and practices his art in Wisconsin.

JAYNE PRENTICE

1971 – 21 years old — Navy Nurse

Many men who were wounded in Vietnam say that the only positive memory they have of their experience is waking up to see a smiling round-eyed woman standing over them. Jayne was one of those women, a nurse on the hospital ship Sanctuary, anchored just off the coast of Vietnam.

"When I was on my way to Vietnam, we had a layover in Los Angeles, and I called my mom. She told me a good friend of mine, who I had just seen, was killed in Vietnam. That brought up such a surge of emotions for me. It made it so real for me at that moment. I guess I was more scared, but also more determined to help."

In spite of her desire to help, she feels guilt that she couldn't do more

"What I saw was nothing compared to nurses in field hospitals, and the guys in combat. My experience there was not all that bad, and I feel guilty I didn't do enough. I wasn't in the jungle, in combat zones, where maybe I could've done more. I was on a comfortable ship with hot showers. I just have a huge amount of guilt."

Many of the patients she had reacted the same way when they got their Purple Hearts.

"Many felt like they didn't deserve it because their wounds weren't as severe as others. Some wanted to go back and fight, some just wanted to go home. Even the guys with severe wounds were more concerned about their buddies, and how they were doing. Some of the ones who were going home were the most depressed, because they knew how senseless the war was, and they were afraid for the safety of the friends they were leaving behind."

Jayne, like so many returning veterans, often found coming home could be an unpleasant experience.

"When I came back and said I was in Vietnam, people would just ignore it. They'd say 'Oh. Nice weather.' Nobody wanted to hear about it, so I just bottled it up, along with most other veterans. I ended up writing poetry about my experience, and I wrote letters to men I lost there. That was my way to try and heal. But I think it was very damaging, being forced to treat it like a secret, having to bury those feelings for all these years. People's attitude towards Vietnam veterans may have caused almost as much damage as the war itself."

Jayne is divorced from her Vietnam vet husband, and still practices nursing.

DAVID ORTEGA SHAW

1969 -70 — 19 years old —Tunnel Rat

D avid was the "little guy", so he was ordered to be the tunnel rat, crawling in holes, looking for Viet Cong.

"It was a job no one wanted, so it commanded some respect, and I had to push myself more. It was exciting. I worked with a Kit Carson scout (a repatriated Viet Cong) who knew the underground system, and taught us how to fight the war, like the US military never did. Soldiers aren't the bad guys. I never killed anyone who wasn't trying to kill me, I never killed an unarmed civilian, I never raped or looted. I fought an honorable war. But I saw the same thing happen to the Vietnamese that happened to our people *(David is Native American and Hispanic)*; burning villages just because the government says so. It was the Indian wars all over again."

"When I came home it was like hurtling into space. I got to my parents' house, and slept three or four days, because I finally was in a safe place. Then I called my girlfriend, and found out she had gotten married, so I got screwed by her, screwed by the government, screwed by everyone. It didn't give me a good reference for being a healthy individual. But I promised myself and her before I went, that I would never love anyone else, so I guess I spent the next 25 years waiting for her, even after I married someone else. My wife was wonderful, beautiful, and bright, but for whatever reason, I couldn't give anything back, and always had other women. I worked hard and brought home a paycheck, but after work, I was crazy; had a bad temper, couldn't sleep without a gun, always anxious, did drugs. It was such abhorrent behavior, and I couldn't figure out why. "

"I thought I was "normal" because I went to college, got a degree, had the same job for 20 years; things most vets with PTSD can't do. I didn't really think there was anything wrong with me, and still don't think there is, in the classic sense. But the only thing I've done since I got out is deal with vets, talk vet stuff, talk Vietnam, so in a sense, I'm still there. Everything I've ever done professionally or spiritually is based on that experience. Not only is it OK in my job to be a Vietnam vet, be a little crazy, it's actually helpful in dealing with clients. It just masked my own symptoms."

"The only thing I can do now is to put my past into perspective and try to have a stable life and relationship, and try to be happy. I'll never be happy in the classic sense, I'll never be the person I was before I left."

"Short of having my kids, my experience in Vietnam was the greatest thing that ever happened to me. MAYBE if I hadn't gone, I'd have gone to law school as I planned, and married my true love, been a great man. But Vietnam is *who I am* to other people, and it's where I get my respect."

David is an instructor and counselor at the Veterans Upward Bound program at Humboldt State University. His students say his greatness lies in the fact that he goes way beyond his job expectations, to befriend veterans and help them set and achieve their goals. "He's got a good heart," says one former student, "and you know he'll never let you down."

HERB MONK

Herb was 17, still in high school, when he joined the Marine Corps.

"One of my friends was getting drafted, so eight of us joined and we all made it back. I got hit four times, got two purple hearts, and was there less than four months when they sent me home. I got hit by an 82 mm mortar, hit all over, except for my head, so I was lucky. But it did hit my carotid artery."

"I was in the hospital a few months, and got about 100 mg of Demerol every four hours, so it's a blur. I was on an amputee ward in the hospital, with some pretty bad cases. They talked a bunch of us gimps into being in this Vets Day parade, put us on a float, and people threw bottles and stuff at us. I knew then it was probably a good idea *not* to tell anyone where you've been."

One injury left his arm immobile, and they wanted to amputate.

"My arm just dangled like a cow's tail. I got electrical stimulation but nothing was working, so I finally convinced a PT guy to jazz the stimulator. He was afraid it might hurt me, but I told him my options didn't look too good, so he did it. Wow! I sort of had contortions, but my little finger on my right hand took off. I saw him twice a day, and my fingers started coming around. It was pretty neat. Then I was discharged."

At home, he was too far from a base to continue PT, so he did his own!

"My trick to do this stimulus was a light switch in my parents house that had a short. I'd lay a wet towel on the floor, grab the light switch with my right hand, then step onto the towel and turn the light on. It'd just about knock me down, so I'd put one foot off the towel at first, to get used to it. But I kept seeing all this progress. I felt pretty lucky.

"I never felt OK to talk about Vietnam until the mid-80's. My friends I joined with, we never talked about it, except one guy who got MS from Agent Orange. I just figured I didn't do anything special. I was retired at 18, with 80% disability, so I just drank, and fished, and knocked around. I found out later that when I was on all that Demerol, it increased my tolerance, so when someone said lets have a couple beers, I figured they meant a couple 12-packs. You drink to alter the mind, so if we're gonna do it, lets get out to where no man's gone before. I wonder what I missed while I was drunk for 20 years."

He met his wife in 1974 after she'd graduated from the University.

"She used to party with us, but then she figured it was time to grow up, and thought I had a problem. I kept drinking and doing drugs until 1992, and finally Sue, her dad, and a close friend, had an intervention with a gal from rehab. I just said "Ok, lets go", and I went through rehab and quit. I'd always said I'd quit when I turned 40, but with my tolerance level being so high, I'd probably drink 15 beers a day. I still go to the bars once in awhile; it's like a therapy session watching those clowns do the same thing I used to do. A friend quit before me, and told me to look honestly at how much I drank. When I figured it out, I took Sue to the train depot, and showed her how much it was; about 2 freight cars full. I was lucky to have a wife who cared."

"I planned to be a smoke-jumper, but when I got injured, the VA said they'd retrain me. I'm in my third year now, taking resource conservation. School is hard, and about my third week, I was wondering if it was gonna work. But then I'd tell myself, hey it can't be that bad; they're not gonna shave my head and make me walk point. I do that before every test."

Herb, who never graduated from high school, has a 3.5 GPA in college, and is considering attending graduate school. He is still happily married.

JIM HENDRIX

3 tours, 1967-71—Army Rangers, Long Range Recon Patrol

*T*he six-man LRRP patrols were tight units. Jim was a squad leader.

"We did ambush patrols and things like, when Tet broke out, we took back the embassy. I was good at my job, so I volunteered for two more tours."

"The shutdown came when we had so many guys bagged and tagged, and they weren't even there long enough to know their name. It'd tear you apart. As a squad leader, I knew when I sent a guy in, he might not come back, but I had to do it, and couldn't ask myself if it was right or wrong. I had to detach. When you killed someone, nothing happened, no court-martial, no jail, and we even said things like neutralize target instead of kill, to make it impersonal. But the bottom line is, you have to live with what you did for the rest of your life. You have to be able to look in the mirror and feel OK, and hope you don't just bubble over one day."

He found when he got out, he was unable to sleep, or even get a job.

"They find out you're a Vietnam vet, and they don't hire you. So I started drifting, eating at missions, following crops, barely making enough to survive, but it was OK. I thought I was going crazy, not sleeping, having all this goin' on in my head, and there wasn't any help then. I got wounded and thought they had to amputate my leg, but they had this radical new procedure and now I'm walking. So they'd take care of your body, but not psychological stuff. I thought I was alone till the 80's. I found a weekly group, and the counselors there sent me to an in-house program for 6 months. I had group and individual therapy, and there was a guy in group I was in Vietnam with, so that was helpful. When I got out, we had a year of follow-up therapy. It was good to get it all out. I still had the nightmares and flashbacks, but could deal with it, knowing I wasn't alone. That's when I started working for Pac Bell, so I have to watch my stress, and be careful I don't go off on anyone. I still have no long term relationships, and I'll never be as close as other people. I just don't have that ability anymore. It's always there; I just don't know what might set me off, or what the breaking point is."

"A few guys from LRRP have committed suicide. They just gave up, can't deal with it anymore. You never know if you'll be the next one. It's always there, and you just try to park it, not let it overwhelm you. But you know if it hits you when you're down, you might lose it.   I try not to think on it, not to get too tired or too stressed, because it'll creep up and grab you. There's no one out here that can really understand it, if they haven't lived it."

Jim was upset when his son enlisted and went to Desert Storm.

"That kicked up a lot of old stuff for me. I went to the airport to meet him when he came home because I didn't want him to be alone like I was."

"Vietnam was where I grew up, where I came of age, where my future was shaped. I can't change it, and I've come to accept my lot. I have to accept myself and what I've done. They say the lucky ones are the ones that didn't come back; it's truly over for them. The rest of us are just here struggling, looking for purpose, wondering why I didn't get killed, why did I come back."

Jim still doesn't sleep, but tries to work nights, so it becomes an asset.

MIKE MC CARTY

1966 — Fourth Infantry

Mike was sent to Vietnam after his first wife turned him into the Draft Board in Seattle the day they got divorced. "I don't feel anger toward her, though. I feel sad, because she's had to live with that for all these years."

"I was in the jungle, in combat 10 solid months. On July 23, 1967, we got hit by 4,000 NVA. First my thumb was shot off, then they got my shoulder, as I dragged a wounded buddy back. The third one was between the eyes, which took out my eye socket, which is why I wear the patch. Apparently my glasses deflected it, so it took out the bridge of my nose and my eye socket, broke my jaw, and came out my neck. I was in the hospital eight months. They gave me disability for disfigurement, and loss of sight and smell, and upped it to 100% based on unemployability. I was a loose cannon for a couple years. I carried a .357, hit the bars a lot, and if anybody messed with me, I just took 'em out. I thought I was fine mentally, but obviously I wasn't."

Then he met his wife, who finally persuaded him to attend college.

"I had the eye patch so I stuck out, and the girls would give me shit about being in Vietnam. The only place where people accepted me was in the bars, so that was a comfortable place to be. The so-called intellectuals and liberals were the ones who were cruel; no one ever spit on me, but I had women lift their butts in the air and fart at me as I walked by, and they said some incredibly cruel things."

"I kept trying to drown it, to get numb, but luckily I became a parole officer in 1972; I saw what chemical abuse was doing to other people, saw guys go to prison for the things they did because of it. One day in 1981, I drove home and didn't remember it. I went out the next morning to check the car for dents, and I thought, "You know, they shot me between the eyes and tried to kill me, and now I'm trying to kill myself. What an idiot." I never had a drop after that. My wife is the one that saved me. She would've left me."

"I work with convicts, so I still have the adrenaline rush, which, regardless of what people say, is unbeatable. It's a good occupation for me because I deal with people that aren't what you call normal, and they're shocked I can think like them. What I went through helps, because these guys respond to someone they think is tougher than them."

"Vietnam was THE turning point in my life. The things I experienced there took my youth and naiveté away from me. I saw a guy get thrown out of a helicopter, a woman beat to death, a woman raped, saw people die, bodies burned with kerosene. You can't go through that and not be changed. It also taught me a lot about myself. I learned that even when I was scared s---less, I still could move and do something. The negative is it scarred me for life, I'll never be the same. It made me a cynic. I'm grateful I survived, but after I saw the things I saw, I question whether there is a God. I'm still wired tight. It showed me what human beings are capable of; people just have no concept of that. I'll probably never get over being angry at the people, how they treated us when we got back. The government always lies, but the treatment by people was shameful. I feel really sad for all the lives lost and damaged. But I don't think one can wallow in self-pity because they got a raw deal."

Mike says he has fewer dreams as the years go by, but thinks he still exhibits all the classic symptoms of PTSD.

"I still feel the effects of it, physically as well as mentally. I still get choked up when I talk about it, and I'll go to the grave never having gotten over it. I've got stuff buried so deep that why would I want to bring it up now? I went a year dreaming combat dreams every night. I didn't go ten minutes without thinking about it. I would just burst out crying. Why would I want to go back in there and drag that back out? I don't think all the counseling in the world will correct that, I don't think any thing will. It's like having one eye, it's just some-thing you live with. I'm pretty much at peace with myself. which is why I hesitated talking to you; once I bring it up, it takes awhile to get it back down again. I'm tired of agonizing over it. I have to move on with my life, and my life is pretty darn good."

Be bold and courageous. When you look back on your life, you'll regret the things you didn't do more than the ones you did.

JEANNIE HASENBECK

1968 — 20 years old – Red Cross, 24th Evac Hospital

*J*eannie has devoted over 30 years of her life to searching for her younger brother Paul, who has been a POW/MIA since 1968.

"I'll never forget it. It was a Sunday morning, and my Dad and brothers had gone to mass. I looked out the window, and saw my father, the parish priest and a military officer. My Dad had tears streaming down his face, so I knew it was bad, but I just never thought anything could happen to Paul. They told us he was missing, but he'd be returned after the war, and we were never to talk to anyone about it. Not to anyone that contacted us, or other families, even families of the three other guys he was missing with. I thought this was unique to us, but I learned many years later, after joining the League of Families, that everyone had been told this. That's how they kept us from getting organized and demanding answers."

She was 20, and Paul was 19 then; she decided she had to look for him.

"I saw an ad for Red Cross volunteers to go to Vietnam, and it seemed faster than going in the military. I didn't tell anyone, but I went for a day-long interview, and they selected me. They said I'd be assigned to SMH (Service to Military Hospitals) and assured me I'd have training when I got there. That night we were at the supper table and I said I was going to Vietnam. There were 10 people at the table, and it was dead silent."

"I'd *never* even been in a hospital, and this was a neurologic and orthopedic center, with head wounds and amputees. My first day, they took me through the wards, and I went out back and just heaved. I couldn't believe what I was seeing. I learned later that even the medical people had trouble with the magnitude of the destruction of humans, but I was totally unprepared for it."

When the war ended, she lived in Denver with a nurse friend from Vietnam.

"We'd been told that when it ended, Paul was coming home, so when they read the list of POWs released by Hanoi, and his name wasn't on it, I thought there must be a mistake. It was like losing him all over again. We thought we'd done all we could, and our government had done all they could. It wasn't till the last five or six years, we realized how much *hadn't* been done, and how much more we *could've* done. Of everything my brother thought could happen to him, he NEVER thought his country would abandon him. But his country did. I love my country but I do not trust my government. The level of deceit and cover-up is astounding. It's prevented healing. Their official report has been that Paul died the day he became missing, but now we know there are too many contradictions for that to be the case. My friend lost her husband, and he was known to have lived in captivity three years. He only had a half-inch thick file, so how could my brother have died the first day and have a 19-inch thick file?"

When she saw a colonel, the curator of a war museum in Vietnam, with Paul's dog tags, her life went into another whirlwind.

"Senator Kerry was there with this guy, who said he wrote a detailed diary of the ambush and execution of Paul and the three men with him, and he could lead them to his gravesite. So I see this on TV! No military warning, nothing. I've got a phone bill of over $800 that night trying to get find that reporter, or anyone who could help me. That started us on the journey we've been on for nearly six years. Today a team left Hawaii for Vietnam, and will hopefully find his remains at the site the Vietnamese told them about. The museum in Hanoi has 13 artifacts of his, and they had the capability to do this all along but they chose not to. The only reason it's gotten attention is when it came time to normalize with Vietnam, certain senators said no, not

Paul

Tom

Daniel

David

until we've accounted for these POWs. So Clinton stood at the Vietnam Memorial and promised he'd never normalize with them until we had all that information, but the very next week, he did it.

There's evidence that some POWs survived long after they were captured, so Jeannie feels Clinton signed a death warrant for anyone still alive at that time, since the Vietnamese had told us they held no live POWs.

"My life since the war has been consumed with Vietnam, and I look at life so much differently since I was there. The first 10 to 15 years, it directly impacted my life every single day, and I've lived my life since then as a result of being there. I never planned to do anything different than what everyone else in Freeburg, Missouri did; get married, and raise kids. But after Nam I couldn't return to all that sameness. I never intended to be single at 53, and had opportunities to marry. But my independence and my exposure to Agent Orange stopped me. I had nurse friends from Vietnam who'd had kids with birth defects, so it was scary to think of having kids with that possibility. To me, kids were the only reason to marry, and if that option was taken away from me, I didn't need it. But I have a very rich life, and value my friends. All my close friends are from Nam. I saw so many people die at 17, 18 years old, that I know how easily life can be taken away. I feel an obligation to live a good life, not only for my brother, but for all the other young men I saw die there. Nam gave me a feeling of satisfaction and self-worth that I've never had since. I wish the war never happened, and I'd never lost my brother and all the other kids we lost, but in some ways a lot of good came out of it for me. I feel like I lost him, but I found me, and I don't know that I would've found me if I hadn't lost him. It was so rewarding, the most satisfying year of my life, even though I didn't find Paul. I'll never do anything to compare with it."

"I was invited to speak about my experience at an organization, and after I told Paul's story the man who had invited me to speak came up to me. He said "That's a very interesting story you told, but I think if your brother didn't come home, it's because he chose to stay behind and enjoy the whores in Saigon". You'd be surprised at the things people will choose to believe, to avoid believing that our government left people behind over there. Even my mother didn't want to believe it. She was a staunch supporter of the government, and it was almost as hard for her to believe they would leave him there, as it was for her to hear that he was missing."

"Until I'm certain he's dead, I have to keep looking. It's been over 30 years, but I can't leave him behind, I can't give up."

There are still over 2,000 missing in Vietnam, and Paul Hassenbeck and his three buddies are among them. These military photos of the four boys, taken in 1968, are the constant reminder to Jeannie of what her year in Vietnam was about. She can never forget, and she hopes the rest of the country will never forget, either.

WEYMOUTH SYMMS

1969 — 23 years old — Swiftboat on Mekong Delta

A sense of duty and honor is what compelled Wey to go to Vietnam, Once you're there, you just try to stay alive. With a 75% casualty rate on the swift boats, I feel guilt I survived when so many didn't. I had four close friends die there."

Wey went over and back with his unit which made it somewhat easier.

"But coming home, we flew into San Francisco, and...I know there's been doubt whether people really got spit on, but it happened to the three of us. The heroes then were the war protesters. I don't criticize their decision, but I'd like the perception to be that *we* made the greater sacrifice. Maybe they have some guilt they didn't support us, so I guess we all have our baggage to carry. But it divided us, and that still needs to heal on both sides."

Peoples' reactions left him confused about the war, feeling he didn't fit in with his peers, so he didn't tell anyone he was a Vietnam vet.

"Sixteen years later, we started a committee to build a memorial for Montana Vietnam veterans, and people were astounded to see me, and all these people they knew for years, who they now find out are Vietnam vets. It was the beginning of our coming out of the closet, acknowledging who we are. Before that, I stuffed it all, and landed in the ER, with a heart attack... which turned out to be a panic attack. It kept recurring, and was humiliating. I think I'm a together guy, able to handle anything, so I just struggled through for years, miserable, afraid to go anywhere if I couldn't get to a hospital quickly. I would've been smarter to get counseling, but it was hard to admit I needed help. I figured I got through the war OK, I could do this. My capacity for stress is less because that war experience is always there, just under the surface. I try not to focus too much on it, and focus on more positive things."

Like the first Swiftboat reunion in D.C. in 1995. There, Wey and his buddies recalled an incident where they bent a few rules to help a lieutenant and his troops who were being overrun by Vietcong. The last morning of the reunion was a Father's Day breakfast. A man approached Wey's group and asked if anyone was on a boat in 1969, describing the incident. When he found it was them he said, "I was the Lieutenant who was getting overrun, and your Swiftboat saved our lives. I've been looking for you guys for 25 years, but you didn't file a report, so I didn't know who you were. I came here hoping to find you."

"We were just blown away. We walk outside and he introduces us to this young woman, and says "I want you to meet my daughter." The daughter hugs me, tears in her eyes, and says, "Thank you for giving me my Dad." So there's some good things to come out of Vietnam. She was so thankful to have her Dad, and I have a bond with them now that is unbelievable."

"Vietnam is the most important part of my life, in defining who I am and what I'm about as an adult. Then, it was 1/23 of my life, and now it's 1/52 so I have a better perspective on it; but it's still the absolute defining experience in my life. In war you've done the most exciting thing you'll ever do and been the most totally alive you'll ever be. It's an exhilarating, terrifying experience; not one I'd like to repeat. I can't imagine how anybody could go through that and not be affected."

Wey is a husband, father, and bank officer, and was one of the people to help make the Montana Vietnam Veterans Memorial in Missoula a reality. He is standing in front of the Memorial here.

ED MILES

Ed trained Vietnamese soldiers to take over during the Vietnamization process. He and his radio man were the only Americans in their unit.

"The Vietnamese were not well trained or equipped, and not really interested in it. It was sad. My radio man got his arm blown off, and I was really upset. Then I was on an operation, trying to get to my wounded point men, when a mortar round went off two feet from me. It blew me 15 feet into the air, and I landed on my back, and couldn't move. I started getting cold in 100 degree heat, I couldn't breathe, I got tunnel vision, and I knew I was dying. I was just really pissed off, not scared or looking back at my life. I got 15 units of blood, and we only have 16 total, so I guess I was pretty bad. My parents got a telegram saying I was seriously wounded and they didn't know if I'd live, then the Army lost track of me and it took them two weeks to find out I was still alive. I don't think my Mom ever got over it. She was never the same after that, it messed her up so bad."

Ed didn't use alcohol or drugs as an escape when he was in Vietnam, but his re-entry was difficult and his recovery was long.

"I started drinking and smoking dope when I was in the hospital. That was our form of therapy, since they didn't offer us any. I was still in the Army then, but I was totally against the war. I did an antiwar interview, and Melvin Laird sent MPs to the hospital to arrest me. I got retired a week later."

"I had so much anger, and drank so heavily, I lost my wife and many of my friends. I finally stopped drinking because of my six-month-old son. I was so fed up with this country, and our government, I ended up moving to Europe in 1979. I got my life together a little more over there, and calmed down somewhat. I met another woman while I was there, and we came back to the States in 1981 and had another son.

"I knew of Bobby Muller through Vietnam Vets Against the War, but when I was on a trip to Vietnam with some other guys, I ran into him in a cafe in Hanoi, and we really got to know each other. I started working with him at Vietnam Veterans Of America in 1989, and that has helped me work through a lot of things."

"One positive thing from all this, is that I'm very close to my kids. When I was living with the Vietnamese, I got to see how much they treasured children, and how well kids were treated in Vietnam, how happy they were, even in war. Part of my coming to terms with how Vietnam changed me, is having my kids be part of it, and helping them to understand my experience there and how it has affected me."

"The humanitarian work that I do here and in Cambodia is tribute to the fact that I want to contribute something positive to people's lives. I was part of something that was incredibly destructive and painful, and this work helps me come to terms with that. I'm still angry, and maybe I always will be, but it's less now because of the work I do."

Ed was wounded April 26, 1969, three days before Bobby Muller, who works down the hall from him at Vietnam Veterans of America Foundation. They come from neighboring towns in New York, but didn't finally meet until after the war.

Ed works with Bobby in Washington, D.C., and makes frequent trips to Vietnam and Cambodia to help carry out the humanitarian work of the organization.

ALEX McELREE

1964-65 and 1968-70 – 19 years old — Navy

*A*lex spent his first tour of Vietnam on a ship, then served two more at the hospital in Da Nang. He was planning to make the Navy his career.

"But my drinking and drug use got so severe, and I got so crazy while I was there, I was afraid they'd kick me out, so I took an honorable discharge and left in 1971, after 8 1/2 years. I don't necessarily put any or all of this on Vietnam; I think I was screwed up before I went, but it got a lot worse while I was there. Maybe they shouldn't have sent a screwed up guy into a war."

After leaving the Navy, Alex stopped drinking. He tried to work, but found it hard to hold a job and was homeless off and on until 1980.

"I spent most of my energy just trying to stay sober. Then I got a job driving ambulance in Oakland, and that brought it all back; in 1981 we had a guy burned on 90% of his body, and I flashed back to a guy hit by Napalm in Nam; it was the same smell, everything. After being sober several years, I took a drink that day, and I drank and was homeless again for four more years."

He again achieved sobriety in 1985, still living in his car. He married a couple of years later, and managed fairly well until he had a heart attack in 1991.

"I was going in for the third time to open the artery, my wife couldn't take it anymore and left, I got lead poisoning and couldn't work, a lot of bad stuff. I just couldn't cope, so I stuck a shotgun in my mouth, pulled the trigger, and it didn't fire. It shocked me, enough to know I needed help. So I called my doctor, who called his therapist, and I saw her until I ran out of money. She saved me. Then I got hooked up with the VA, and was in combat focus group, where I got the idea to start this place *(a homeless shelter).* It was Christmas, and a guy from Khe Sahn was homeless, and it really upset me. I said somebody should do something about it, and he said why don't you? So I got a landlord to rent me this old house cheap, I took my Social Security money and bought beds, and I brought home some vets. That was the beginning."

"My doctor had a fit; they said I couldn't work, and they were gonna try and get me 100% disability so I could sit and vegetate someplace. But the less I did, the more suicidal I got. Once I got my teeth into something and got going, the fight in me came back. I wasn't gonna let Vietnam beat me."

Since 1993, Alex has welcomed home hundreds of homeless vets through Operation Dignity, working seven days a week, always trying to do more for them.

"It gives me a purpose in life. We give them a safe place to live and good food, we get them help for alcohol and drugs, and mental illness, and we hold them accountable for their actions. Over 50% of the vets who come here stay sober, and get their lives together. I tell them it's time to get right with it, quit blaming Vietnam, stop hurting. We say "Welcome home," and remind them they once wore a uniform and put their life on the line for their country; we give them back their dignity. We have to believe in each other, and hold each other up. And we have to want help. I love what I do, but I do it to kill the pain, 'cause I still think of suicide every day. I don't know how much is Vietnam, and how much is I'm just nuts. I don't think you're born this way, but somewhere along the line it went really bad for me."

"I feel responsible for other people's pain, and think it's my fault, Vietnam was my fault. So I have to constantly tell myself I didn't turn my back on them, I didn't hurt them. But in a way I did, being drunk. So this is my way of making up for it. I want to leave my mark, something that says my life did make a difference, it was important. "

"My guilt is that I didn't die there, my name isn't on the Wall. Instead of dying a hero, I came back a failure, a common drunk. I finally made it to the Wall, and I was able to spend a lot of time there, and cry, and say I'm sorry. And this shelter is my way of saying I'm sorry, I didn't forget you. A symbol we use is the POW/MIA; it represents my feeling that I'll never forget, and I won't let America forget, that we left these people behind. I still get very sad about the way vets are treated, and that so many are homeless and people don't care. Shame on this country for letting this many veterans go homeless. So my lot in life is to do my little bit for them. I can't give them much, but I give them all I've got."

"For awhile, I wanted to hold onto my anger and hatred and guilt. I didn't want to let go of the pain. I'll never forget it, and I'll probably never forgive my country for doing this to us, but I can't get caught up in that; it distracts me from my mission, which is to get them off the street. We're not gonna leave our people on the battlefield, and we consider the streets the battlefield. But I know that some of them are never coming home."

He now has 80 housing units, and big plans for helping even more vets

"I own six lots on this block, debt-free, and I started from nothin'. We have drawings done, and we're gonna knock this building down and build 48 or 68 units of housing. We'll open a detox, a multi-service center. When we tear these buildings down, part of our history goes away, but then it'll really represent what I want Operation Dignity to be, which is something fresh and new and beautiful and homey. It's kind of a before and after, the same thing we're trying to do with our lives. We're the failures of the world, the winos and drunks and homeless. Nobody wants us in their back yard, but look what we've been able to accomplish."

"The biggest fear I have, is that I'll be homeless again. I know this could all be gone tomorrow if I take a drink. When I was sober before, I would've never thought I'd take a drink, but now I know it can happen. If I don't keep doing what I'm doing I could take a drink, or more likely, do myself. I work on that in therapy, twice a week, trying to eliminate suicide as an option."

"I don't wanna run around in camouflage greens and be pissed off anymore. All it does is hurt me. I think the fight is starting to go out of me. I'm more into making a difference than fighting with everybody, and I'm not as ashamed of who I was or what I did. I was dealt a hand and didn't play it very well, so now I have another chance at life, another hand to play. It's up to me if I want to be angry and feel sorry for myself, or I can be an active part of the community and make a difference in what happens to me, and what's gonna happen for the vet that comes behind me. I never turn anyone away."

JIM CORR

1968 — 19 years old — Army

"Till that day I never treated it as reality, I wasn't really there. On this mission, all hell broke loose. A guy got hit, so I called the medic, then *he* got killed; everyone was killed. So I put this guy on my back and crawled. To get over a rice paddy dike, I rolled him off and jumped over. I pulled him up, straining and yelling (mouth open) and I got hit. The bullet went in my mouth and out my neck, and I couldn't move. Jimmy, a neighbor from Long Island was there, but I didn't know it; they flew another platoon in when we got wiped out. He saw me get hit and threw a smoke grenade to mark that I was alive, so he saved my life, and *he* got shot when he threw it. The only way I found out was he told people back home what happened. I was in the hospital 14 months, so he got back first, and I saw him when I got home, but we never talked about that day *(he began to sob, unable to continue for several minutes)* I never talked about this...I don't know if I can do this...I just never talked to him about it. I saw him before I moved; he just sat in the bar every day. I said I was fixing my car and driving to Colorado, and he said, "Why? The inside of one bar is the same as any other." That's the only time I ever talked to him, and we never talked about that day, or him saving my life."

Jim left New York for a new life in Colorado, got a job at a bar in the mountains, then ended up owning it. He liked being in control of his life.

"I could blow up the road on both sides of the bar, and be king of the mountain! If I wasn't in control, I never would've made it. I called it the 'freedom bar', where people could do whatever they wanted; smoke pot, get wild, anything. So I drank and partied, too busy to deal with any Vietnam stuff. I did OK till one 4th of July. I saw a thing on Vietnam and it was like I had a flashback or an out-of-body experience, and for a week I was just gone. It was almost 20 years to the day since I got shot, so I guess I blocked it out for all that time. My injury was so bad I was focused on trying to heal my body. I had small episodes before, but nothing like this. When it hit me I was in the shower; I got out and couldn't leave my room. Days later I tried to go to a market, and it was like people weren't really there. Someone talked to me, and I saw their lips move, but I couldn't hear them. I went to a shrink in Cheyenne, and had to wait in the hall. I freaked out, I was totally disoriented, a mess, didn't know where I was, or what to do. I'm not dealing with my PTSD at all now. It seems to be OK unless I have a lot of stress."

"Right now my stomach is in knots. I thought I could handle it, but I just don't talk to people about Vietnam, not even other vets. I couldn't even tell people about the day I got shot for many years. I do have crises when I have stress. Sometimes I'll get up in the morning and just cry when I'm by myself. I don't usually do what we just did, and cry in front of anyone else. I feel very inadequate about it sometimes; I feel like I should be able to handle it."

"My wife said I was crazy for doing this. But I hope some good comes of it. I hope other vets look at it and say hey, we're not back there, and it's a big wonderful tomorrow. If you feel sorry for yourself, you lose. There are times I have weird thoughts, but my wife has been great support, and stayed with me through all this. People need to know what life is like for a Vietnam vet, not just think we're all screwed up. I don't care what I look like, or if my speech is messed up, I just want to live. No matter how bad things get, I know they'll never be that bad again. When I'm feeling down it's hard to think that way, but I think it made me stronger and was positive overall."

Jimmy has now sold his businesses to spend more time with his wife and daughter.

BOBBY MULLER

September 1968 to April 1969 – 23 years old - Marine Infantry Officer

"**B**eing a great athlete was the most important thing to me in college, followed by how to make lots of money. I had no political consciousness, but I bought the government rhetoric about repelling a communist invasion, so I enlisted in the Marines right after college. I was happy to serve my country."

Vietnam changed Bobby's life in ways he never could have imagined. While leading an assault, he was hit by a North Vietnamese bullet that entered his chest, went through his lungs, then severed his spinal cord.

"I knew, beyond any doubt, that I was going to die. I was never more sure of anything. I was laying on the ground, looking up at the sky, and I could actually feel the life leaving me. It was a peaceful feeling, but my only thought was, I didn't want to die alone. That's why waking up on the operating table was so spectacular, so incredible. When I realized I was alive, I thought I was the luckiest man on the planet."

Then the doctors told him he was paralyzed from the waist down.

"I read my hospital records after I was discharged; they said that if I had arrived just one minute later, I'd have been dead. One minute! I never had one single thought about what I had lost, I thought only 'My God, I'm alive!'"

The first time he cried was experiencing the subhuman conditions at the VA hospital in the Bronx, NY, during his rehabilitation. When he was discharged from the hospital in June 1970, he became active in the anti-war and veteran's rights movements, then went to law school so he could do more. He planted himself where he could do the most good, in the middle of the political arena in Washington DC.

"So I went from a business major, wanting to make big money, to only thinking of how I could help other people. Working with the Paralyzed Veteran's Association, and being in that situation myself, I realized how badly Vietnam vets had gotten screwed on all types of readjustment benefits. It was obvious the government was not going to take care of veterans as they had promised, so we had to do it for ourselves. I lobbied and got the first hearings on PTSD and Agent Orange, problems that the VA wanted to ignore. Then we founded the Vietnam Veterans of America in 1979 to help vets get the benefits they were entitled to. In 1989, I founded the non-profit Vietnam Veterans of America Foundation (VVAF), which is now acknowledged as one of the world's leading humanitarian organizations, providing prosthetics and rehabilitation services to victims of war in Vietnam, Cambodia, El Salvador, and Angola."

"I'm a very lucky man. Going to Vietnam changed my whole direction in life, I became a completely different person. My life has been much more fulfilling because of my experience there."

In 1991 Bobby helped establish the International Campaign to Ban Landmines (ICBL), with VVAF serving as coordinator. In 1997, Bobby Muller and other representatives of VVAF went to Oslo, Norway, to accept the Nobel Peace Prize for the campaign efforts.

The names of the dead are read at the traveling Vietnam Memorial Wall.

The occasion was the 30th anniversary of the Summer of Love in San Francisco's Golden Gate Park. At one end of the park the traveling replica of the Wall was set up. People walked slowly along the length of the Wall, stopping to look, to touch, to weep, to sit in silence. Some talked in hushed tones, some hugged. Few smiled.

At the other end of the park, vendors sold tie-dyed clothing and other '60s memorabilia, bands from the era such as Country Joe and the Fish, blared out their tunes, and the now-middle-aged anti-war protestors spoke to a cheering crowd. People danced, laughed, and participated in the usual fair activities, an air of merriment pervading.

There still seemed to be a division between those who went, and those who didn't. But now there was something everyone could agree on. People at both ends of the park spoke of how wrong the war was, how wrong the government was, to waste all those young lives. They all agreed that the sacrifices made by the Vietnam Generation should never have been. Everyone, whether protester or veteran, wished they could go back to the '60s and make it all different.

As the sun rises at the Vietnam Memorial Wall, casting its warm light on the names of all the young lives lost, and all the lives between the lines that were forever changed, let us open our hearts to a new day, a new way of looking at these lives.

Let this be a day for the Vietnam Generation to heal, for a nation divided to become a people united. A day for all of us to forgive ourselves, and forgive each other. A day to see that those stories between the lines may be those of your neighbor, your co-worker, your child's teacher, your local policeman, your brother or sister

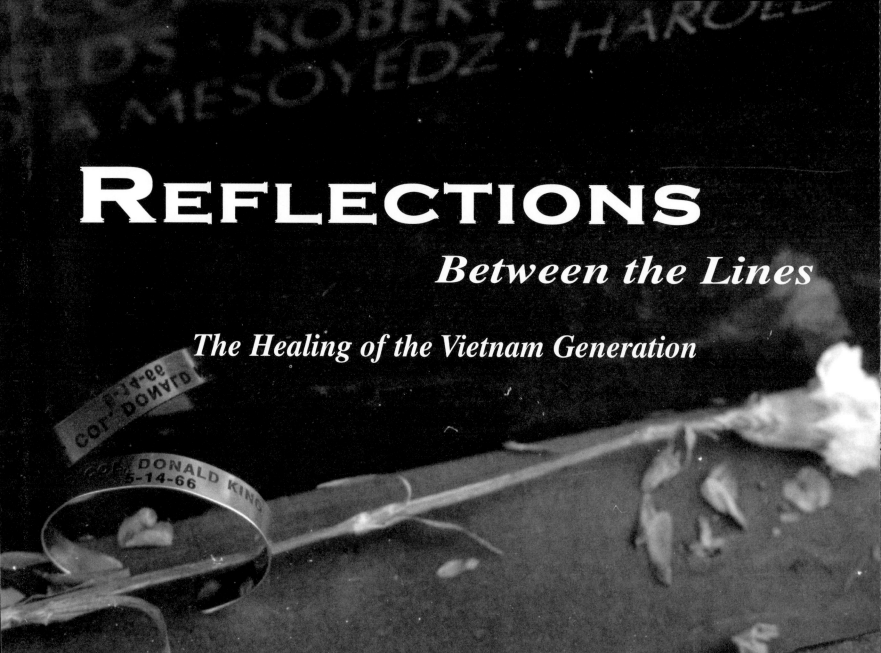

REFLECTIONS

Between the Lines

The Healing of the Vietnam Generation